By Robbin F. Laird

TRAINING FOR THE
HIGH-END FIGHT

THE STRATEGIC SHIFT OF THE 2020'S

CONTENTS

This book is dedicated to Edward Timperlake,
whose passion and knowledge of all things military
have taught me more than I can ever repay.

And with regard to life and its struggles,
he has been an inspiration.

PREFACE

2020 has been a very dynamic year, with significant global changes, many of those associated with COVID-19 and its ripple effects. We are publishing a separate book which deals with those changes, and is entitled. *2020: A Pivotal Year?* In this book, I have focused on another major aspect of our work during 2020, namely, the further adaptation and evolution of the U.S. forces in preparing for conflict in a contested environment, variously referred to as the return of Great Power Competition, peer conflict, or the high-end fight.

The majority of the book focuses on what was learned from a number of visits and discussions at warfighting centers in the United States during visits over the past few years, with the bulk of the interviews included in the book coming from visits this year. These visits have been to Norfolk, Virginia; Jacksonville and Mayport, Florida; San Diego, California; and Las Vegas and Reno, Nevada.

Because travel has been limited this year, the visits take on more significance. We want to bring our findings to as wide an audience as possible with regard to how rapidly the U.S. air, maritime, and ground forces are adapting to the new strategic situation. We have interviewed the practitioners of the art of delivering a more capable combat force NOW and not in the mists of future time.

The book starts by providing a brief overview on the strategic shift and the crafting of the integrated distributed force to be able to deliver effective outcomes for our political leaders. We have a book being worked currently on maritime kill webs and deterrence to be published by USNI press which lays out in detail how the way ahead is being shaped with regard to the crafting and operations of the integrated distributed force.

The setting is then in place to discuss what it means to train for the high-end fight. To train for and execute the capabilities of the high-end fight requires that training and exercises be well funded, and the innovations being generated by the warfighting centers drive force structure development.

The force that is evolving is a very capable one, but the reset in its combat approaches and combat architecture is crucial to enhancing its capabilities to provide for the skill necessary to master the puzzles and challenges of escalation management and to shape the skills needed for the world we are now in.

The book is built around the interviews conducted in 2020 and, in some cases, from past visits. The dates indicated are when the original article was published on *Second Line of Defense* or *Defense.info*. Most of those interviews were conducted by me, but the past visits have been done with my colleague Edward Timperlake.

INTRODUCTION

The U.S. military has been focused along with core allies in dealing with counter-insurgencies for two decades, which represents a defining generation of combat experience for the joint, and coalition force. We have an entire generation of military officers with little or no experience in dealing with the direct threat from peer competitors or operating in contested air and maritime space.

With the return of great power conflict and the return of core nuclear questions with the coming of a second nuclear age, force structures are changing along with concepts of operations as well as the need for relevant and effective crisis management strategies. A strategic shift is underway for the military establishments in the liberal democracies.

For the past decade, the military has primarily focused its training and operations dealing with counter-insurgency and stability operations. Now the need to deal with operations in contested air and sea space from adversaries that can bring significant capability to bear against U.S. and allied forces requires a significant reset of efforts.

It is a strategic space in which operations by the military will unfold in contested settings over an expanded combat space. It is about learning how to deal with the policies and capabilities of peer competitors who are seeking strategic and military advantage against the liberal democracies. And this challenge is one which will require the civilian leadership to come to terms with the challenge of crisis management in which escalation and de-escalation will have to be mastered as a strategic art form. It will not just be combat effect sought; but crisis management effects as well.

It is not just about sending off the military to fights thousands of miles away and welcoming them back from time to time. It will be about facing the adversary squarely and forcing his hand and shaping outcomes to the benefit of the liberal democracies against those of the illiberal powers, and by doing so with using military means as one of the key tool sets

The nature of the threat facing the liberal democracies was well put by a senior Finnish official: "The timeline for early warning is shorter; the threshold for the use of force is lower." What is unfolding is that capabilities traditionally associated with high-end warfare are being drawn upon for lower threshold conflicts, designed to achieve desired political effects.

Higher-end capabilities being developed by China and Russia are becoming tools to achieve political–military objectives throughout the diplomatic engagement spectrum. The non-liberal or authoritarian powers are clearly leveraging new military capabilities to support their global diplomacy to try to get outcomes and advantages that enhance their position and interests.

The systems they are building and deploying are clearly recognized by the Western militaries as requiring a response; less recognized is how the spectrum of conflict is shifting in terms of using higher-end capabilities for normal diplomatic gains.

As the strategic shift from the land wars gains momentum, the investments and training in an appropriate twenty-first century crisis management and high intensity combat force will not be modeled on the Cold War European-based force. It is not about a German–U.S. Army brotherhood with significant presence. It is not about reestablishing air–land battle. It is about leveraging core force integration capabilities, such as F-35 with the Aegis, which can provide a pull function moving the United States and the allies toward a more flexible and scalable force that can operate across the spectrum of operations.

Because the adversaries are building to mass and are emphasizing their expansion of strike capabilities controlled by a very hierarchical command structure, the kind of force which will best fit Western interests and capabilities is clearly a distributed one. Fortunately, the technology is already here to move effectively down this path, a path which allows engagement at the low end and provides building blocks for higher end capabilities.

The force we need to build will have five key interactives capabilities:

- Enough platforms with Allied and U.S. forces in mind to provide significant presence;

- A capability to maximize an economy of force with that presence;

- Scalability whereby the presence force can reach back if necessary, at the speed of light and to receive combat reinforcements;

- Be able to tap into variable lethality capabilities appropriate to the mission or the threat in order to exercise dominance; and

- And to have the situational awareness (SA) relevant for proactive crisis management at the point of interest and an ability to link the fluidity of local knowledge to appropriate tactical and strategic decisions.

The new approach is one which can be expressed in terms of a kill web, that is United States and allied forces so scalable that if an ally goes on a presence mission and is threatened by a ramp up of force from a Russia or China, then that presence force can reach back to relevant allies as well as their own force structure to deliver the appropriate response.

The inherent advantage for the United States and its allies is the capability to shape a more integrated force which can leverage one another in a crisis. A shift to a kill web approach to force building, training, and operations is a foundation from which the United States and its allies can best leverage the force we have and the upgrade paths to follow.

A kill web linked force allows a modest force package—economy of force—to reach back to other combat assets to provide for enhanced options in a crisis or to ramp up the level of conflict if that is being dictated by the situation.

The evolution of twenty-first century weapons technologies is breaking down the barriers between offensive and defensive systems. Is missile defense about providing defense or is it about enabling global reach, for offense or defense? Likewise, the new fifth-generation aircraft has been largely not understood because they are inherently multidomain systems, which can be used for forward defense or forward offensive operations.

Indeed, an inherent characteristic of many new systems is that they are really about presence and putting a grid over an operational area, and therefore they can be used to support strike or defense within an integrated approach. In the twentieth century, surge was built upon the notion of signaling. One would put in a particular combat capability—a Carrier Battle Group, Amphibious Ready Group, or Air Expeditionary Wing—to put down your marker and to warn a potential adversary that you were there and ready to be taken seriously. If one needed to, additional forces would be sent in to escalate and build up force. With the new multidomain systems—fifth-generation aircraft and Aegis, for example—the key is presence and integration able to support strike or defense in a single operational presence capability. Now the adversary cannot be certain that you are simply putting down a marker.

The strategic thrust of integrating modern systems is to create a grid that can operate in an area as a seamless whole, able to strike or defend simultaneously. The US Navy (USN) leadership has coined their version of this approach, the "kill web."

In an interview we conducted with Rear Admiral Manazir, then head of N-98, Naval Aviation, he discussed the new approach. "If you architect the joint force together, you achieve a great effect. It is clear that C2 (command and control) is changing and along with it the CAOC (Combined Air and Space Operations Center). The hierarchical CAOC is an artifact of nearly sixteen years of ground war where we had complete air superiority; however, as we build the kill web, we need to be able to make decisions much more rapidly. As such, C2 is ubiquitous across the kill web. Where is information being processed? Where is knowledge being gained? Where is the human in the loop? Where can core C2 decisions best be made and what will they look like in the fluid battlespace?

"The key task is to create decision superiority. But what is the best way to achieve that in the fluid battlespace we will continue to operate in? What equipment and what systems allow me to ensure decision superiority? We are creating a force for distributed fleet operations. When we say distributed, we mean a fleet that is widely separated geographically capable of extended reach. Importantly, if we have a network that shares vast amounts of information and creates decision superiority in various places, but then gets severed, we still need to be able to fight independently without those networks.

"This not only requires significant and persistent training with new technologies but also informs us about the types of technologies we need to develop and acquire in the future. Additionally, we need to have mission orders in place so that our fleet can operate effectively even when networks are disrupted during combat; able to operate in a modular-force approach with decisions being made at the right level of operations for combat success."[1]

Inherent in such an enterprise is scalability and reach-back. By deploying a digital warfare grid or a C2/Information superiority "honeycomb," the shooters in the enterprise can reach back to each other to enable the entire grid of operation, for either defense or offense. By being able to plug into such a digitally enabled honeycomb, the United States provides force augmentation and surge capability to those allies and at the same time those allies enable forward deployments which the United States would not own or operate.

Put in other terms, presence is augmented at the same time as scalability is as well. This provides a significant force multiplier across the crisis management spectrum. In a kill web enabled force, every shooter is a sensor; and some sensors as shooters.

---

1   Robbin Laird and Ed Timperlake, "The Deputy Chief of Naval Operations for Warfare Systems Looks at the Way Ahead: Rear Admiral Manazir on Shaping Kill Webs," *Second Line of Defense* (October 13, 2016).

In effect, what could be established from the United States perspective is a plug-and-play approach rather than a push approach to projecting power. The allies are always forward deployed; the United States does not to attempt to replicate what those allies need to do in their own defense. But what the United States can offer is strategic depth to those allies. At the same time, if integratability and interactive sustainability are recognized as strategic objectives of the first order, then the United States can shape a more realistic approach than one which now rests on trying to proliferate power projection platforms, when neither the money nor the numbers are there.

The training function is changing dramatically as an integrated distributed force is being shaped, battle tested, and further developed. The U.S. military is not just sitting around waiting for the force of 2030 or 2040 to show up. The focus is upon innovation in shaping a more lethal and capable force now and in the near to mid-term. The cycle of operations-training-development and back again is a key driver for change. In this book, we address the training piece in that dynamic cycle of change.

CHAPTER ONE:

THE STRATEGIC SHIFT

P rior to visiting the various warfighting centers included in this book, a number of interviews conducted over the past few years provide a good overview to how training is changing. The first interview took place in February 2020 and occurred with three senior U.S. Admirals and highlighted how training was in transition. The second was with the Air Warfare Center, Nellis AFB and was conducted in May 2020. In a round table discussion, with Ed Timperlake and myself, a senior USAF officer highlighted how things had changed since he first came to Nellis in 2006. The third interview was with the surface warfare training community where the evolving role of the surface warfare community in delivering integrated effects to the distributed force was highlighted. The fourth interview was with the former Chief of the Royal Australian Air Force, Air Marshal (Retired) Geoff Brown, and he highlighted how fifth generation capabilities were driving change in the training function. And finally, an interview with Air Vice-Marshal (Retired) John Blackburn highlighted how training can drive development in the period ahead.

Shaping the Skill Sets for the Twenty-First Century Fight

February 23, 2020

The strategic shift from the land wars of the past two decades to preparing for the high-end fight is having a significant effect on the dynamics of change affecting the very nature of the C2 and ISR needed for operations in the contested battlespace. An ability to prevail in full spectrum crisis management is highlighting the shift to distributed operations but in such a way that the force is integratable to achieve the mass necessary to prevail across the spectrum of operations.

Much like the character of C2 and ISR is changing significantly, training is also seeing fundamental shifts as well. For the USN, training has always been important, and what is occurring in the wake of the changes in the national security strategy might appear to be a replication of what has gone down for the past twenty years; but it is not. In fact, it is challenging to describe the nature of the shift with regard to training.

With the introduction of new technologies into the fleet, ranging from the new capabilities being provided for the integratable air wing, to the expanded capabilities of the surface fleet with the weapons revolution and the evolution of the maritime remote extenders, to the return to a priority role for ASW with the submarine fleet and the maritime reconnaissance assets working together to deliver enhanced capabilities to deter and to defeat adversarial subsurface assets, the dynamics of training change as well.

Clearly, the training mission is evolving to prepare for the high-end fight, and indeed, preparing to operate across the spectrum of crisis management. But how best to describe the kind of evolution training for the fleet is undergoing?

In a visit Norfolk in February 2020, there was a chance to discuss with three Admirals the shift in training. The host for the meeting was Rear Admiral Peter Garvin, and he invited two other admirals as well to the discussion. The first was Rear Admiral John F. Meier, then head of the Navy Warfare Development Command. The second was Rear Admiral Daniel Cheever, then Commander, Carrier Strike Group FOUR.

The ability to operate across the full spectrum of crisis management highlights the central contribution which the Navy-Marine Corps team delivers to the nation. Operating from global sea-bases, with an ability to deliver a variety of lethal and non-lethal effects, from the insertion of Marines, to delivering strategic strike, in the era we have entered, the capabilities which the Navy-Marine Corps teams, indeed all of the sea services, including the

Military Sealift Command and the USCG, provide essential capabilities for the direct defense of the nation.

One key challenge facing training is the nature of the twenty-first century authoritarian powers. How will they fight? How will their evolving technologies fit into their evolving concepts of operations? What will most effectively deter or provide for escalation control against them?

There is no simple way to know this. When I spent my time in the U.S. Government and in government think tanks, I did a great deal of work on thinking through how Soviet and Warsaw Pact forces might fight. That was difficult enough, but now with the Chinese, Russians, and Iranians to mention three authoritarian regimes, it is a challenge to know how they will operate and how to train to deter, dissuade, or defeat them.

A second challenge is our own capabilities. How will we perform in such engagements? We can train to what we have in our combat inventory, we can seek to better integrate across joint and coalition forces, but what will prove to be the most decisive effect we can deliver against an adversary?

This means that those leading the training effort have to think through the scope of what the adversary can do and we can do, and to shape the targets of an evolving training approach. And to do so within the context of dynamically changing technology, both in terms of new platforms, but the upgrading of those platforms, notably as software upgradeability becomes the norm across the force.

The aviation elements of the Marine Corps-Navy team clearly have been in advance of the surface fleet in terms of embracing software upgradeability, but this strategic shift is underway there as well. The Admirals all emphasized the importance of the learning curve from operations informing training commands, and the training commands enabling more effective next cycle operations. In this sense, training was not simply replicating skill sets but combat learning reshaping skill sets as well.

The Admirals underscored that there was a sense of urgency about the training effort understood in these terms, and no sense of complacency whatsoever about the nature of the challenges the Navy faced in getting it right to deal with the various contingencies of the twenty-first century fight.

The Navy has laid a solid foundation for working a way ahead and that is based on the forging of an effort to enhance the synergy and cross linkages among the various training commands to work to draw upon each community's capabilities more effectively.

Specifically, NAWDC (Naval Air Warfare Development Center), SMWDC (Naval Surface and Mine Warfighting Development Center), UWDC (Undersea Warfare Development Center), NIWDC (Naval Information Warfare Development Center), and exercise and training commands, notably Carrier Strike Groups FOUR and FIFTEEN, are closely aligned and working through integrated operational approaches and capabilities. The synergy across the training enterprises is at the heart of being able to deliver the integrated distributed force as a core warfighting capability to deal with evolving twenty-first century threats.

There are a number of key drivers of change as well which we discussed. One key driver is the evolution of technology to allow for better capabilities to make decisions at the tactical edge.

A second is the challenge of speed, or the need to operate effectively in a combat environment in which combat speed is a key aspect, as opposed to slo-mo war evidenced in the land wars.

How to shape con-ops that master C2 at the tactical edge, and rapid decision making in a fluid but high-speed combat environment? In a way, what we were discussing is a shift from training preparing for the next fight with relatively high confidence that the next one was symmetric with what we already know to proactive training for problem solving for a fluid, contested battlespace. How to shape the skill sets for the fight which is evolving in terms of technologies and concepts of operations for both Red and Blue combat forces?

In short, the Navy is in the throes of dealing with changes in the strategic environment and the evolving capabilities which the Navy-Marine Corps team can deploy in that environment. And to do so requires opening the aperture on the combat learning available to the fleet through its training efforts.

The Perspective from the Air Warfare Center, Nellis AFB

With Ed Timperlake

May 21, 2020

We visited the USAF Warfare Center in 2015, when Major General Jay Silveria was the commanding officer. Now because of COVID-19 restrictions, we visited "virtually."

In a round table via teleconference on May 12, 2020, we discussed with the Air Warfare training center the training focus. We discussed this issue with the following officers: Colonel Jack Arthaud, Commandant of the USAF Weapons School (USAFWS), Lt. Col. Ethan Sabin, Commander of the 6th Weapons Squadron, and Lt. Col. James Combs, Commander of the 8th Weapons Squadron, Major Peter Mattes, Director of Operations, 19th Weapons Squadron.

We started by asking Col. Arthaud how the training approach being pursued currently differed from his earlier experiences. "In a word, I would say integration. Clearly, what has evolved is a much more challenging and complex air warfare environment. We have shifted from a primary focus on training to execute de-conflicted operations or parallel operations, to higher levels of teaming, higher levels of group coherency and integration, because that's what the threat demands.

"When I was a student in 2006, the twenty-two-week course spent twenty and half weeks on individual weapon systems expertise with the remainder on collaboration. Our way of war then was focused on de-conflicted air warfare or sequential air operations, As an F-15C operator we would focus on doing our air sweep and then there would be follow up strike packages and then a wide variety of support assets in the air operation.

"We were not an integrated weapons school but we added a number of elements, such as the Mobility Weapons School, and a full complement of air, space, cyber, and special operations platforms, all resident in the Weapons School today which facilitate training for integrated force packaging.

"And with the shift to deepen integration, our integration phase of training is now six of the twenty-two weeks compared with the week and a half I went through as a student fifteen years ago. With this has come a shift in the skill-sets we prioritize and develop. What it means to be credible has changed over the last fifteen years.

"At that time, being credible really meant being the best fighter pilot in your aircraft or being the best tactical C2 controller, as examples. And now what we've seen is that there's a need for leadership of the integrated force.

"There's an increased need for critical thinking and problem solving. There's a need to understand the capabilities of your platform in depth—not only so you can optimize the employment of your own platform, but so you can understand how best to combine your platform with others, to best to accomplish the functions and tasks that are necessary to solve the tactical problems facing the integrated force."

The Colonel provided a very clear differentiation between then and now, and in the discussion, which followed, we discussed a number of key aspects of the approach being shaped now in close interaction with the other warfare centers which are operating in relative close proximity, namely, USN NAWDC, and the USMC MAWTS-1. In fact, officers are embedded from each of these centers within each other's centers as well.

We identified a number of key takeaways from the discussion, with some extrapolations from those takeaways along the way as well.

The first takeaway is that clearly the services are working dynamic problem-solving approaches.

They are dealing with evolving adversary capabilities and approaches, and the services clearly are not assuming that they "know" in advance what will be experienced the battlespace. The warfighting centers are cross-learning with regard to anticipated threats, tactics, and challenges rather than coming up with single service solution sets. A very different training regimen is required for force integration to shape a force designed almost on the fly to operate against an evolving threat environment.

At Nellis, they are focusing on effects-based training where the focus is upon problem solving to achieve a specific effect required for specific tactical operational settings. As one officer put it: "We're trying to train our weapons officers, our instructors, and our operational Air Force officers to be able to adapt effectively in a period of uncertainty or in a fight with more uncertain terms. I think that we need to be prepared for some technological surprises that might occur and we need to train to that reality."

The officer added: "We don't know for sure exactly what we might see, but let's go ahead and make some reasonable guesses about what a difficult task or problem might be, and then let's allow our instructors and our students to innovate and try to go solve that forward-looking tactical problem."

The second takeaway is that the USAF is clearly leveraging what fifth-generation capabilities can provide for the joint force. During our 2015 visit, the first F-35 for the Weapons School had just arrived and Major General Silveria had recently become the first USAF general officer to complete qualification training in the F-35. Now with the three services each operating the jet, they are working the significant integration opportunities which flying the same aircraft provides across the force, but remembering that the USAF has forty years of experience in flying low observable aircraft, a legacy experience which provides certainly a leg up on global adversaries, if leveraged properly in the training and operational arenas.

The third takeaway is clearly that the team is thinking in kill web terms, or in terms of an integrated, distributed force. They are working closely with the USN in terms of shaping how distributed maritime operations can come together most effectively with the USAF's evolving airpower distributed operations capabilities as well.

And with the USMC able to shape a very flexible mobile basing capability on the kill web chessboard, shaping ways to maximize the capabilities the individual services bring to the fight, but to do so through interactive sensor webs to shape effective distributed strike is an evolving focus for force integration. And for distributed operations to work effectively, one of the challenges is finding ways to enhance C2 capabilities at the tactical edge and resident in mobile bases to support the overall integrated force.

The fourth takeaway is that the objective is clearly to have greater capability to operate through what is be labelled the advanced battle management system (ABMS). But in many ways, the force is already doing so through the capabilities already fielded and being shaped on the training ranges.

One officer referred to ABMS as the available battle management systems which is a good way to differentiate between the training for the fight, we are in now versus a world in 2030. "The best way I would characterize how C2 has changed in the last decade is less vertical orientation and more horizontal feeders out there in order to create our own web of information sharing with what I term the current ABMS, which is the available battle management system."

The fifth takeaway is how training for distributed integrated operations is yielding innovative ways to operate which have strategic consequences. Too often, it is assumed inside the beltway that operations and tactics are on a level distinctly different from the strategic level, thereby easily missing the kinds of innovations going on at Nellis and its sister warfighting training centers. The kind of kill web integration which is being shaped now and with the addition of new capabilities in the near and midterm has a strategic consequence. For example, the challenges China presents to the United States and our allies in the Pacific requires that air and maritime domains partner well. Working to shape how to partner effectively at the tactical level in a kill web approach allows the United States and its Allies to keep the Chinese off balance and not allow them to prepare for a one attack vector combat situation.

We want adversaries to have to confront a much wider variety of potential dilemmas that we could throw at them. For example, the USN and USAF are working closely together in the electronic warfare domain. The

state plans to employ a range of cyber capabilities to undermine the confidentiality, integrity, and availability of Western allied information in competition and combat."

Because of this situation several key training questions need to addressed and answered. The three key questions for Brown are as follows:

1. How to train in a battlespace saturated by adversary cyber and information attacks?

2. How to exploit the advantages of cyber in multidomain operations?

3. Do we have the tools and key infrastructure to train in an appropriate manner?

"I believe it's safe to say it is impossible to deny an adversary entirely of the ability to shape aspects of the information environment, whether it's through spoofing or sabotaging ICT-based warfighting systems. As a result, our goal should be to sustain military operations in spite of a denied, disrupted, or subverted information environment."

He underscored the challenge this way: "The requirement is that warfighters need to be able to fight as an integrated whole in and through an increasingly contested and complex battlespace saturated by adversary cyber and information operations. But how to do this so that we are shaping our con-ops but not sharing them with an adversary in advance of operations? The battle for information control needs to drive our training needs much more than it does at the moment. We need to provide warfighters with the right kind of combat learning."

We then discussed current approaches such as at Red Flag and how we might change the approach to get closer to the kill web capability. "During large-scale exercises like Red Flag, cyber training is often employed in parallel with traditional kinetic training programs and is not fully integrated. Non-cyber war fighters do not necessarily experience the effects of "cyber play" while it is ongoing.

"When cyber effects are integrated into live training events, my experience is that they are often "white carded." Although this does provide war fighters some insight into how their systems or platforms may be affected in the event of a cyberattack, the lack of realism precludes them from experiencing and subsequently troubleshooting that attack."

He cautioned that there are good reasons why this is not done. "The integration of these effects into a live training environment could sabotage the other goals of the exercise, present safety risks to war fighters, and reveal platform vulnerabilities to inquisitive adversaries." In spite of the limitation, "these live training challenges can't preclude us from training for a future contested and complex battlespace."

He argued that "We definitely need to train as we fight—so we need to develop tactical level cyber and information effects for simulators and to develop adversary cyber and info effects into our evolving concepts of operations."

In other words, Brown argued that live training remains very significant for organizing a strike and defense force and working the physical pieces of the task force or air group. But the virtual world is now a key area in which you will shape, work on and exercise your information force concepts of operations.

"One of the foundational assumptions I've always had is that high-quality live training is an essential to producing high-quality war fighters but I believe that's changed. Even if you don't take cyber into account, and look at an aircraft like an F-35 with an the AESA radar and fusion capabilities, the reality of how we will fight has changed dramatically. In the world of mechanically scanned array radars, a 2v 4 was a challenging exercise—now as we have moved more towards AESAs where it is not track while you scan, but its search while track, it's very hard to challenge these aircraft in the live environment. And to be blunt about it, the F-35 and, certainly the F-35 as an integrated force, will only be fully unleashed within classified simulations. This means that we will achieve the best training outcomes for aircraft like the F-35 only if we have a more comprehensive virtual environment."

If we do not do this, we will fly fifth generation aircraft shackled by legacy air combat approaches; and we will not unleash the kill web in terms of its complexity and lethality unless we shape a training approach which allows the F-35 working with other key force elements to deliver a kill web outcome.

Building in Integration

September 8, 2017

The Australian Defence Force has set a tough bar for itself—shaping an integrated force and crafting an ability to design such a force. This is a tough bar but one which they are trying to energize in part by leveraging their new platforms to shape a way ahead beyond the classic after-market integration strategy. But how best to do this with regard to training and development of the force? And how to maximize the combat effectiveness to be achieved rather than simply connecting platforms without a significant combat effect?

A major opportunity is uncovered as the training approaches, capabilities, and technologies change. Notably, it is possible to shape a capability to connect training, notably cross platform training with software code rewriting of the sort, which the new software upgradeable platforms like F-35 clearly can allow.

During a 2017 visit to Canberra, I had a chance to discuss with Air Vice-Marshal (Retired) John Blackburn how the training approach could be expanded to encompass and guide development.

"We know that we need to have an integrated force, because of the complexity of the threat environment we will face in the future. The legacy approach is to buy bespoke pieces of equipment, and then use defined data links to connect them and to get as much integration as we can AFTER we have bought the separate pieces of equipment. This is after-market integration and can take us only so far. This will not give us the level of capability that we need against the complex threat environment we will face. How do we design and build in integration? This is a real challenge, for no one has done so to date?"

Laird: "And the integration you are talking about is not just within the ADF but also with core allies, notably the United States forces. And we could emphasize that integration is necessary given the need to design a force that can attack an adversary's military choke points, disrupt them, have the ability to understand the impact and continue on the attack."

"This requires an ability to put force packages up against a threat, prosecute, learn, and continue to put the pressure on. Put bluntly, this is pushing SA to the point of attack, combat learning within the operation at the critical nodes of attack and defense and rapidly reorganizing to keep up the speed and lethality of attack.

"To achieve such goals, clearly requires force package integration and strategic direction across the combat force. How best to move down this path?"

Blackburn: "We have to think more imaginatively when we design our force. A key way to do this is to move from a headquarters set requirements process by platform, to driving development by demonstration.

"How do you get the operators to drive the integration developmental piece? The operational experience of the Wedgetail crews with F-22 pilots has highlighted ways the two platforms might evolve to deliver significantly greater joint effect. But we need to build from their reworking of Tactics, Techniques, and Procedures (TTPs) to shape development requirements so to speak. We need to develop to an operational outcome; not stay in the world of slow-motion requirements development platform by platform."

Laird: "Our visit to Fallon highlighted the crucial need to link joint TTP development with training and hopefully beyond that to inform the joint integration piece. How best to do that from your point of view?"

Blackburn: "Defence is procuring a Live/Virtual/Constructive (LVC) training capability. But the approach is reported to be narrowly focused on training. We need to expand the aperture and include development and demonstration within the LVC world. We could use LVC to have the engineers and operators who are building the next generation of systems in a series of laboratories, participate in real-world exercises.

"Let's bring the developmental systems along, and plug it into the real-world exercise, but without interfering with it. With engagement by developers in a distributed laboratory model through LVC, we could be exploring and testing ideas for a project, during development. We would not have to wait until a capability has reached an 'initial' or 'full operating' capability level; we could learn a lot along the development by such an approach that involves the operators in the field.

"The target event would be a major classified exercise. We could be testing integration in the real-world exercise and concurrently in the labs that are developing the next generation of 'integrated' systems. That, to my mind, is an integrated way of using LVC to help demonstrate and develop the integrated force. We could accelerate development coming into the operational force and eliminating the classic requirements setting approach.

"We need to set aside some aspects of the traditional acquisition approach in favor of an integrated development approach which would accelerate the realisation of integrated capabilities in the operational force."

CHAPTER TWO:

NAWDC SHAPES A TRANSITION

Overview

The Naval Aviation Warfighting Development Center or NAWDC is best known to the public as "Top Gun." Prior to June 2015, the center was called Naval Strike and Air Warfare Center (NSAWC). But today's NAWDC is significantly different from that public perception of the fighter pilot gunslinger. NAWDC has led a coordinated effort within the Navy to rethink how to train for the "high-end" fight and how to reshape its force to do so within the joint warfighting context.

We have visited, Fallon Naval Air Station four times. The first visit was when Rear Admiral Scott Conn was the CO and that was in 2015. The second visit was when Rear Admiral Harris was the CO and that was in 2017. And the two visits in 2020 were with Rear Admiral Brophy as the CO of NAWDC. The second visit was to observe Resolute Hunter, which is a Navy-led joint ISR exercise, which is working thorough the ISR/C2 transformation underway as the kill web approach takes hold.

These visits underscored the transition underway for the Navy to deal with the strategic shift. It is clear in retrospect that Rear Admiral Conn was laying the foundation for significant change. The recognition of the need for a significant shift in warfare was becoming evident, with changes in the tactical and strategic environment.

The visit in 2017 highlighted how the Navy was reorganizing its warfare centers to reshape how to operate in the new strategic situation. During that

2017 visit we noted: "Since we last visited the training command, the name has changed and that change reflects a broadening of the focus to both infusing the Navy with an evolving aviation approach and integrating the air wing with the broader challenges occurring within the fleet. It is about preparing for the integrated high-end fight and the NAWDC captures that demand signal. And with the arrival of software upgradeable aircraft, like Advanced Hawkeye and F-35, it will be increasingly important to put the evolving TTPs or Tactics, Techniques, and Procedures as part of the software code rewriting effort as well."

In 2020, a set of interviews were generated in the Spring prior to a July 2020 visit. This allowed for some in-depth looks at the way ahead at NAWDC. But the focus is very clear for NAWDC. Rear Admiral Brophy noted: "Admiral Miller gave me the following charge when I took command: 'Snap', when you go there get us in a great power competition mindset. From a wholly integrated perspective, look at what we need to do at NAWDC in order to win the next fight. And to do this he emphasized that my job was to pursue holistic training with the Navy and to work with other U.S. warfighting centers and key allies."

We now turn to the overviews by the Commanding Officers at NAWDC in 2014, 2017, and 2020 and then to a more detailed look at the developments underway at NAWDC in 2020.

The Perspective of Rear Admiral Scott Conn

With Ed Timperlake, November 4, 2014

As we concluded our visit to The Naval Strike and Air Warfare Center, we had a chance to discuss the Center and the way ahead with Rear Admiral Scott Conn, Commander of the Center. The Admiral noted that the "mission we have here started with TOPGUN, forty-five years ago. TOPGUN was founded out of failures in combat during the Vietnam War. TOPGUN training led to measurable improvements in Air to Air kill ratios. Through the years, other communities have mirrored the TOPGUN model including the

EA-18G HAVOC course, the E-2 CAEWWS course, and the H-60S/R SEAWOLF course.

"These courses target advanced training at the individual level. Additionally, as a result of failures in combat in Lebanon, STRIKE University, now call simply Strike, was stood up in 1984 to target training at the integrated warfighting level. We have learned a lot of lessons at Fallon and we have had a lot of time to shape an effective combat learning environment. Bottom line, my job here is to prepare our forward deployed air wings to fight and win in a wide variety of missions across the globe."

Question: You have focused on counter-insurgency missions a great deal in the past decade, but clearly the next will return you to high-end warfare and the challenges of dealing with denser defenses and fighting in contested air space. How are you preparing for those contingencies?

Admiral Conn: "There are clear challenges in terms of fighting the high-end fight in the period head. And if you look at the map in front of us which shows our ranges in Fallon in terms of miles, depth, and breadth, it is clear that I am running out of real estate (land and airspace) to train to the entire kill chain of integrated fires."

Question: We have seen a similar situation with MAWTS at the Yuma Marine Corps Air Station as well, and they expanding their operational area by using other ranges such as at Nellis or the Goldwater Range near the Luke AFB.

Admiral Conn: "We work in close coordination with our counterparts in Nellis. We maximize every opportunity to work together in developing joint solutions to the high-end fight of the future. Through the process we better understand the capabilities the joint force brings to bear, and develop the tactics, techniques, and procedures (TTPs) to fight jointly.

"But this issue of training to the high-end fight is not only about real estate, it is also about our desire to not reveal to potential adversaries how we intend to fight. These considerations are driving us to live, virtual, and constructive training solutions as part of our overall operational training environment game plan. Let me be clear, as far as I can see there will always be a requirement to conduct training in aircraft.

"At Fallon, in addition to developing and practicing those TTPs to fight and win in any scenario, we also provide the opportunity to stress the various systems with end to end live fly validation. As an example, when a mission is planned that requires the delivery of ordnance, whether that ordnance be bullets, bombs, or missiles, sailors have to build up the weapons, then the weapons are loaded on an aircraft; sailors then have to check to see that the aircraft can communicate with the weapon, then aircrew have to preflight the aircraft, take off, fly to the range, conduct airborne system checks, fight their way to the target, arm the aircraft, hit the pickle, and, in most cases, guide the weapon to the target.

"This is a brief description of the kill chain that ends up in a kinetic effect, or to state clearly, a bomb going high-order on the target, and the right target at the right time. This live fly validation cannot be done in a simulator. That said, in a simulated environment, I can have aircrew jump in a device, and I can train them at the integrated level across the entire kill chain for various missions. I can conduct this high-end training very quickly, a lot of reps and sets if you will, at reduced cost."

Question: How do you develop your evolving anticipated threat environment?

Admiral Conn: "Future threat assessments are developed collaboratively between Office of Naval Intelligence, Fleet and Combatant Commanders, Naval Air Warfare Resource Sponsors, and Naval Air Systems engineers. This process includes input from NSAWC's subject matter experts. While NSAWC participates in this process, our main focus is to be able to fight and win today with today's equipment. Additionally, I need to be clear that NSAWC is one part of the Fleet Response Plan.

"The training we conduct at Fallon is from the fights on to the knock it off, and is not focused on taking off and landing on an aircraft carrier. The fact that Naval Forces fight forward from the sea is what makes us unique and provides our Nation with the presence to prevent crisis, and if required, to respond to a crisis quickly and decisively.

"The cold hard truth is that launching from a Carrier, or one of our Amphibious Ships for our Marine Corps brethren, is inherently dangerous and unforgiving of mistakes or complacency. This unique maritime operational aspect is addressed through follow on training by Carrier Strike Group (CSG) 4 and CSG 15 who make recommendations for certification for deployment."

Question: We found it interesting that your strike integration training involves as well regular dialogue with the deployed carriers and apparently you work in support of the deployed fleet as well in shaping TTPs, which they might need in ongoing operations. Could you speak to that process?

Admiral Conn: "NSAWC innovates in peacetime while providing the reach back support to adapt in war. We are in regular communication with the deployed carriers. We provide technical and tactical reach back support to address observed shortfalls in combat to existing TTPs.

"An historical example of how NSAWC provided reach back support to the forward deployed warfighter was in the early stages of Afghanistan operations. Ground commanders needed aircraft to strafe at night. To do this strafing mission at night, aircrew needed to put an airplane below mountaintops, perhaps in a valley, provide bullets precisely and then pull off target, and not fly into the terrain.

"When NSAWC got this request, in a matter of weeks because it wasn't overnight, a couple weeks, we came up with the tactics, techniques, and procedures for the fleet to execute that mission. We then folded those TTPs into our training for follow on deployers. And the connectivity we have with the fleet through modern communications allows for an ongoing combat learning process between Fallon and the fleet and this flow of information is central to the process of training in the twenty-first century."

Question: Clearly, shortfalls in flight hours and training is a crucial concern for you. How do you view the challenge?

Admiral Scott Conn: "Naval aviation is very interdependent on how we train aircrew and how we resource to those training requirements. As competing readiness requirements pressurize the flight hour program, a bow wave is created by pushing training qualifications later on in one's aviation career.

"Naval aviation is looking at this issue hard, to ensure our future forward deployed leaders will have the requisite knowledge, skills, and experience to in fact, lead. What we will not do, let me repeat, not do, is to lower our training and readiness standards.

"In the future, the live, virtual and constructive training is envisioned to relieve some of this stress, particularly as aging aircraft and fifth-generation aircraft are more expensive to operate.

"Bottom line here is that training is the essential glue for operational success. In combat, you're not going to rise to your level of technology or the capabilities of your opponent, you're going to fall back to your level of training. Today and in future, with the proliferation of precision across the globe, the difference between winning and losing is/will be measured in seconds, not minutes…"

Question: A number of analysts have focused on the Anti-Access Area Denial threat as a serious limiting factor for future USN operations. How do you view that and focus upon how to best train to deal with those threats?

Admiral Scott Conn: "I think it important to emphasize that adversary A2AD capabilities pose a serious threat not only to Navy, but to our entire joint ability to fight and win. For me, it is about expanding the battlespace and training with regard to how to do this. We are developing the means to push out the battle space and our ability to find, fix, track, target and engage the threat. The F-35 will bring enormous capability in this area.

"At the same time, we are developing means to deny, degrade, or delay a potential adversary's ability to do the same to us. This is why the EA-18G with Next Generation Jammer is so important to the Air Wing of the future, with its ability to provide operating sanctuaries for our forces through exploitation of the EM spectrum.

"That said, the proliferation of precision across the globe compresses engagement timelines, things will happen very fast. And we have to push those boundaries out to buy freedom of maneuver, decision space, and time.

"We are adding new capabilities to do so in the period ahead. With the advent of a live, virtual and constructive training environment we will then integrate those new capabilities to train and fight in this expanded battlespace. With regard to building out our Virtual Constructive Training, it is a work in progress and one which is central to future of training here at Fallon."

Question: You have been at the command for six months; when you leave the command what do you hope to have achieved?

Admiral Scott Conn: "First and foremost is to continue to provide trained and ready aircrew to operate forward. In looking to the future, in five years we are going to have JSF in the fleet. In five years, we may have UCLASS on our carriers. In five years, the Super Hornet of today is going to be different. In five years, the E-2D capabilities and our networks will have matured. In five years, the threat is going to change and competitors will have more capability.

"In working with Naval Aviation Leadership, we are on a journey of discovery of how to best create a training environment that replicates potential adversary's capabilities. Before I leave, I would like to hand my relief a destination to drive to in this regard."

The Perspective of Admiral "Hyfi" Harris

With Ed Timperlake, August 9, 2017

Since we last visited the training command, the name has changed and that change reflects a broadening of the focus to both infusing the Navy with an evolving aviation approach and integrating the air wing with the broader challenges occurring within the fleet. It is about preparing for the integrated high-end fight and the NAWDC captures that demand signal.

And with the arrival of software upgradeable aircraft, like Hawkeye and F-35, it will be increasingly important to put the evolving TTPs as part of the software code rewriting effort as well.

Admiral Harris, the CO of NAWDC, emphasized the need to resource fully the training cycle by which he meant having the current operationally ready assets in the hands of the warfighters so that they could from the outset train effectively for deployment on the carrier. He highlighted that there were two barriers, impeding the ability to get to an optimum training rhythm. The first might be called readiness shortfalls. "The Navy's tiered readiness system, necessary in the current fiscal environment, has peaks and valleys in the training cycle. So you'll come out of a maintenance phase and you'll be at the low end of your training. We need to make sure that as soon as you go into the basic phase, you have every aircraft that you are authorized to have, and every aircraft has every system that it's authorized. We want to be able to start the training right away, so that you can build reps and sets over time, versus the peak of coming here, getting reps and sets, and then slowing back down again.

"What we've found lately is that as squadrons are coming through, they're about half a step, half a cycle behind. They're not going into Basic Phase with their full kit. Therefore, when they go to their Advanced Readiness Program, they're still getting up to speed. When they come to Fallon, they're still learning some of the things they should have learned in the Advanced Readiness Phase. And then when they go on to their Composite Training Unit Exercise (COMPTUEX) and marry up with the ship and the strike group, they're still learning things that they should have been hard-wiring in Fallon. And we're having to pass those gaps, if you will, onto the next piece of the training track. Readiness should be thought of as investing, the more you can do earlier, and allow that training to compound, the better of you are in the long run, particularly for the high-end fight."

The second challenge is having the most advanced equipment being used in the fleet available to NAWDC. "If I had my way, we would have E-2D here at Fallon. We would have the most current Super Hornet. We would have F-35 on the line. We already have Growler, and our Growlers are operating with the same systems as the latest coming off of the line. And they would have all the systems necessary for our schoolhouse instructors to be out there on the cutting edge of developing tactics. And currently we're doing it piecemeal. We are playing pickup sticks when we need to shape a more capable operational force with our TTP development here at NAWDC."

The enhanced integrated training and development is at the heart of preparing the fleet for higher tempo operations. We discussed this development in two ways. First, NAWDC is working very closely with the surface warfare training community and the Air Force in shaping a more integrated combat training perspective which needs to become more significant in shaping development as well.

With regard to the surface warfare community, the Admiral emphasized the following: "We have surface warfare officers here at NAWDC. We work closely with the Surface Warfare training community as well in shaping a more integrative and integrated approach as well."

With regard to the USAF and integrative training, the Admiral focused on the Growler training with the USAF. "Our HAVOC team works with the USAF Weapons School in the Weapon School Integration phase which runs about a month. If you want to think of it in the college realm, this is a 400-level class. And we're seeing the Growler used differently by the Air Force than we would probably use it in the Navy. That cross-pollination has been extremely useful for both the services."

"Second, the F-35 is a very different type of combat aircraft, and it would be good to see pairings of that aircraft with Advanced Hawkeye and the Growler to shape the evolution of information dominance operations, as a very clear outcome of working these advanced platforms together to deliver evolving combat capabilities. I would like to have advanced Hawkeyes, F-35s and Growlers all here so that we can work integrated TTPs to shape a more effective way ahead for the operational capability of the fleet. I would like to get those type model series weapons and tactics instructors cross-pollinated even more, so that the classes and the courses are integrated more fully than they are now.

"We'll have to find different ways to do that because of the Navy's carrier cycle; we are not resourced to be able to do an air wing and do full Weapons and Tactics Instructor classes at the same time. We have to keep those separated. I'd like to move closer to the USAF model, but we don't have that flexibility because of the carrier operational cycle."

NAWDC will expand its work on integrated warfare by being able to use new facilities being built that will integrate the platform simulators and allow for integrated training and operational thinking at NAWDC. "We are building an integrated training facility. We're going to have all of our simulators under one building, under one common security environment, so that we can do planning, briefing, execution, and debriefing all under the same security umbrella with the full team. The demand signal is that we all need to work together; and the new buildings are being built to meet that demand signal."

"These new facilities will allow for the growth of live virtual constructive training (LVC), although this LVC approach is in its infancy but will become more significant to combat development and training efforts over time. Integrative and interactive training is a key element of shaping a more capable twenty-first century combat force."

One element leading to greater success in this effort is a more integrated air and surface warfare community. As the Admiral put it: "The Surface Warfare Officer (SWO) boss, Admiral Rowden, has been pretty adamant about the benefits of their Warfighting Development Center, the Surface and Mine Warfighting Development Center (SMWDC). SMWDC has been, in my mind, going full bore at developing three different kinds of warfare instructors, WTIs. They have an ASW/ASUW, so anti-surface and ASW officer. They have an Integrated Air and Missile Defense (IAMD) officer and they have an expeditionary warfare officer.

"Admiral Rowden talks about distributed lethality and they are getting there rapidly. We are watching young lieutenants share with their bosses in a training environment, specifically during IADC (Integrated Air Defense Course). This is probably not the way we want AEGIS set up, or how we want the ship to be thinking in an automated mode. We may not previously have wanted to go to that next automated step, but we have to because this threat is going to force us into that logic. And you're seeing those COs, who were hesitant at first, say, 'Now after that run in that event, I get it. I have to think differently.'"

A second element is building out training ranges in a key area of operations, namely, the Pacific. "We do need to continue, to work beyond Nellis, beyond Yuma, beyond Fallon, we've got to start looking at what could we do in Alaska, how can we make Alaska and the events that we do in Northern Edge, more robust? What kind of systems, what kind of sensors, whether it's the Tactical Combat Training System or the ability to go back and replay an event up at Alaska? Or look at Guam as a graduate-level training area, what could we do in Guam when you've got all those assets that are there from both the Air Force and the Navy. How much more could you do in and around Guam? What could you do in Australia, with an ally who is very forward-leaning in technology and integrating with the USN and the USAF, and the way they are integrating their armed forces together? Where can you take advantage of those opportunities?

"All while understanding that as you do that, you are practicing or playing in somebody else's backyard, and they are watching what you're doing. How do you do that, where you can be watched? And what do you have to reserve for places where you're less likely to be watched?"

A third key element is working cross-platform integration to shape a more effective approach to information dominance. "How do I use the capabilities in the F-35 to enhance what I get out of that fourth-gen platform? And, in ways that you didn't think you were going to do it before. Not just by being a bigger, better brother that's going to take care of you on the playground.

"But how do I pass information, what information needs to be passed, and when does it need to be passed? When do I have to be that white knight on the charger coming in to rescue you, to get you back on a timeline, and when can I just sit back and play maybe quarterback or coach and just suggest, 'look here, look there, do this, don't worry about that' threat? And the integration of how do I use that system and the capabilities in the F-35 with those that are in the Growler, where are they complementary? Where are they different, and mutually supportive? In the times that we have had the E-2D out here, how can I work all of those things together?"

And the evolution of LVC will play an important part in the combat development training process. "LVC affords you that environment where you can do the very high-end warfare in an environment where you are not going to be observed. And you can integrate with your surface counterparts; you can integrate with your Air Force counterparts. That linkage is going to be phenomenal. Because now we'll be able to go from F-22s, Air Force F-35, anything else they want to throw in the mix, all the way to AEGIS Baseline 9. And some of those can be live and some can be virtual. And we can go execute. I think that's exciting.

"When you can have a submarine launch a simulated TLAM that's being tasked by an Mobile Operations Center (MOC) somewhere else, that gets a real- update from an actual F-35 flying on the range, that is seeing that the target that you thought was at point A has now moved to point B and you go back through the MOC to go through the firing unit to give that TLAM an updated target, that is powerful."

Throughout the interview and in earlier conversations with the Admiral, the evolving man-machine relationship as a foundational element was discussed in several ways. The Chief of Naval Operations (CNO) has highlighted the importance of enhancing the ability to leverage the man-machine relationships, notably with regard to preparing and executing high tempo and high-intensity operations.

Nothing ever fully substitutes for time in the air. Consequently, the evolving ability to meld flight simulator training beyond the traditional emergency procedures or simulating mission flying is now being developed as a dynamic "man–machine" learning process. Now those pilot and aircrew specific data points can be put into simulators, thus allowing real time repeat learning on how to be a better and better combat team. The Admiral stressed it will be an exciting time as the new facilities come on line for both aircrews and commanders to specifically hone combat skills.

Clearly, the leveraging of the new platforms built around this relationship such as the F-35 and P-8 is important, as well as the capability to build out LVC and integrated simulation to train more effectively are key developments. Above all, what the Navy is looking at are ways to shape new capabilities for learning and the ability to leverage machines to get better fidelity for learning.

The Admiral highlighted another aspect of this process when he discussed the need to enhance the ability to customize learning to repeat specific skill sets for warriors rather than having to repeat whole simulated courses. "We are looking to improve simulated learning for targeted skillsets, and individualized learning over all. And one way you can do that is what they're already seeing in the helicopter simulators, where the helicopter pilot is learning how to hover. And the simulator is assisting them as necessary to make the hovering more successful. As the pilot gets better, the learning software in the simulator backs out and allows the pilot to continue on their own. They get in the simulator the next day, the simulator knows who that person is, knows what they needed the day before, maybe backs that off a little bit to see if they've learned anything. And then brings it back up. So you have the simulator actually assisting with the learning. And they're seeing that people are learning to do skills like hovering faster."

The final subject we discussed is the close linkage between Fallon and the operational fleet in terms of developing TTPs on demand from the fleet as the fleet is engaged in operations.

One example was working TTPs for air combat strafing in Afghanistan as a carrier was about to engage in this task. "For example, we needed the ability in the mountains to do strafing at night because of the proximity of the threat and wanting to have a low threshold for civilian casualties met by using the gun on the Super Hornet and the Hornet. Very quickly NAWDC developed a methodology for night strafing, and it was developed, put right back out to the fleet, and executed within months."

Another recent example was reviewing TTPs after the shootdown of a Syrian jet in the Middle East and working through the mission and sorting out any improvements in TTPs, which might need to be developed. After an extensive review, none were deemed necessary to be made. "The skillsets that we learned in the Advanced Readiness phase, and in Air Wing Fallon, and in COMPTUEX, were everything that we needed to be able to execute the mission we did in Syria."

In short, NAWDC is a new type of combat training development command, which will be increasingly integrated with other warfighting development centers in building the warfighter for twenty-first-century combat operations. But it won't happen without the right kind of investments, the right kind of shifts in mindsets and getting away from the platform centric mentality. And its full impact will be seen when TTPs can be key drivers of development, software and shape modernization requirements going forward.

The Perspective of Rear Admiral Brophy

August 3, 2020

The USN is in the throes of reworking its capability to prevail in the high-end fight while ensuring its ability to engage in full spectrum crisis management. As the center of excellence for Naval aviation training and tactics development, the NAWDC works to ensure an effective, integrated, and lethal force to prevail against increasingly sophisticated adversaries. In a way, with the coming of a new generation of aircraft, Advanced Hawkeye, Triton, P-8, MQ-25, and F-35, the reach of the carrier air wing is beyond the range of the integrated air wing. And NAWDC is an epicenter of practical ways to build out today's navy into an effective integrated distributed force capable of operating as interactive kill webs delivering effective strike, defense, and deterrence against adversaries in the global "commons," as it used to be called.

The discussion with Rear Admiral Brophy, the CO of NAWDC, started with a simple question: "Obviously, NAWDC is in significant change, and your job seems to be to expand the dialogue between NAWDC and the rest of naval warfighting centers as well as the USAF and the USMC and with allies. How would you describe your job?"

Rear Admiral Brophy: "Admiral Miller gave me the following charge when I took command: 'Snap', when you go there get us in a great power competition mindset. From a wholly integrated perspective, look at what we need to do at NAWDC in order to win the next fight. And to do this he emphasized that my job was to pursue holistic training with the Navy and to work with other U.S. warfighting centers and key allies."

In other words, NAWDC is focused on training the integratable air wing. The platform-centered warfighting courses have focused more broadly on the coming of new capabilities and integratability as well as establishing two new non-platform centric warfighting courses, namely, Maritime Intelligence, Surveillance, Reconnaissance (MISR) and Information Warfare.

During the July NAWDC visit, several key developments stood out. First, there is a re-imaging of the carrier going on associated with the return to blue water operations and rethinking how the carrier works with the fleet to deliver enhanced expeditionary reach that the carrier air wing can support. This has meant a growing working role with the Marines, who in Rear Admiral Brophy's words "have significant experience and expertise with expeditionary operations, and with whom we can collaborate to develop new concepts of operations." Rear Admiral Brophy underscored that there was clearly an enhanced working relationship with MAWTS-1 at Yuma MCAS going on as a result.

Second, this has meant that the USN and the USAF are establishing new ways to work more effectively together.

Third, the theme of integratability beyond the carrier air wing is a key one being worked at NAWDC. As Rear Admiral Brophy put it: "From a training standpoint, we work from the perspective of 'it is not going to be a carrier strike group that wins the next fight on its own, it's going to be an integrated joint force that wins the next fight. We've really broadened our aperture. Everything we do here now is based off of a single lens: does it move the needle for great power competition or not?"

Fourth, an integrated training center has been built from the ground up to support the integratable air wing to train in the kill web space. After the interview we toured the new facility which consists of two buildings. The first building is a meeting center with areas for working groups to meet at various levels of security within a global teleconferencing framework, as the need demands. This building can allow for scenario generation, assessment of findings, and evaluations from the physical test range, or utilization of the simulated test range that is contained in the second building

The second building houses multiple simulators for different platforms being flown by the fleet. As Rear Admiral Brophy put it: "We're going to put in an entire Air Wing's and strike group's worth of simulators." The focus is not only on platform learning but also, significantly, on working in an integratable environment. Those specific simulators, continued in various rooms in the building, can be linked with outside simulation facilities as well.

As Rear Admiral Brophy put it about the new facilities and their contribution: "The Integrated Training Building will be the future of virtual and constructive training for the majority of naval aviation. Not only will we provide cutting-edge training in Fallon, but fleet concentration areas will be able to train remotely with the Subject Matter Experts (SMEs) at NAWDC in a virtual, constructive environment at any time, day or night."

Fifth, even with the new facility, changes are necessary with the physical ranges to adjust to the high-end training of fifth-generation warfare. There are requests in to adjust the ranges to accommodate the kind of targeting challenges which the high-end air arm needs to train for to prevail in the high-end fight.

As Rear Admiral Brophy put it: "Fallon is the only United States Navy facility where an entire air wing can conduct comprehensive training while integrating every element of air warfare. While aircraft and weaponry have evolved substantially in the last several decades, the ranges at Fallon have not changed significantly in size since 1962. Our naval aviators use the desert skies to learn critical warfighting skills necessary to defend our nation and preserve our way of life from those who would want to cause us harm. To that end, we are working with the local community, as well as natural and cultural resource experts, to find a way forward together to expand the range."

Sixth, a measure of the change at NAWDC has been the generation of working groups based at NAWDC that reach out to the fleet to devise and implement new ways to operate in the evolving strategic situation. COVID-19 has slowed down this process, but the trajectory is clear. For example, in the first quarter of 2020, NAWDC sponsored work with the other Navy warfighting centers to address the question of fleet-wide TTPs to execute maritime strike. The purpose is to think beyond the classic airwing focus to a wider integratable air wing in support of fleet-wide operations. Clearly, the new infrastructure highlighted above would be a key asset in shaping such new TTPs for the fleet and its integratability into the joint and coalition force.

Seventh, the new MISR or Maritime ISR warfighting center is managing an important new Navy exercise, Resolute Hunter, which is focused on the evolving role of ISR and sensor networks in guiding C2 and integrated operations going forward. The second such exercise was held in November of this year, and included USMC and USAF elements as well.

As Rear Admiral Brophy put it: "In the Resolute Hunter exercise, we are really looking hard at the Kill Web aspect and focusing on utilizing every asset that's out there to ensure that we're the most effective warfighting force we possibly can be."

Taken together, the work of MISR, the Information Warfare program, Resolute Hunter, and the work with the Marines and the USAF, highlights the challenge and opportunity for shaping a Maritime Squadron Targeting Concept. This is a clear expression that NAWDC and the Navy are focusing on ways to leverage an integratable air wing for the fleet, and for the joint and coalition force. As Rear Admiral Brophy put it: "What exactly do twenty-first-century fires look like from a maritime perspective?"

Eighth, Rear Admiral Brophy underscored how important it was to ensure kill web capabilities and effectiveness. A distributed fleet without integratability delivered by interactive kill webs would weaken the force. It is crucial to ensure that a distributed force has ready access to fires across the joint and coalition force to ensure combat dominance.

In short, NAWDC is a key epicenter where the current force is becoming more capable and lethal, and the aperture of the integratable air wing has been opened to provide a key venue for the kind of force transformation needed for full spectrum crisis management dominance.

Redesigning the Strike Syllabus at NAWDC

During a visit to NAWDC in early July 2020, there was an opportunity to continue discussions begun earlier in the year with the CO of NAWDC and his senior officers. Rear Admiral Brophy had highlighted as one major change at NAWDC was the complete revamping of the strike syllabus at NAWDC. And he credited the work of CDR Papaioanu (N-5 Strike Department Head) with leading the effort in re-designing the strike syllabus. Prior to becoming the N-5 Department head, he was the CO of TOPGUN, which was a normal progression at NAWDC.

CDR Papaioanu underscored that "this was the first major rewrite of the strike syllabus at Fallon in more than twenty years." This was being driven by the shift from the land wars to great power competition and the need to operate in a fluid extended battlespace. As he put it: "The level of modern warfare is nothing like we have seen before. We are talking about extraordinarily intense capabilities across a broad spectrum of warfare." How to fight effectively in such conditions? According to CDR Papaioanu: "The key to the modern fight is an ability to integrate an effective force package."

The strike syllabus has been redesigned to work a combat force able to "integrate an effective force package." Clearly, the coming of the F-35 is part of the technological stimulus to such a rethink and redesign. But it is also part of a significant change in how C2 and ISR is being used to shape the approach to strike as well. As discussed with CDR Fraser, head of the information warfare department, dynamic targeting is a key capability which the fleet needs to be able to deliver.

The new strike syllabus is designed in large part to deliver a dynamic targeting capability.

According to CDR Papaioanu, the redesign was driven by inputs from the theater commanders with regard to what they wanted from Naval Aviation in the context of the strategic shift to the high-end fight. Based on feedback from the theater commanders, they began the process of reworking the curriculum. He and his team worked closely with COCOM planning staffs in thinking through the redesign.

The fleet is a key enabler of combat flexibility. "We are the 9/11 force for the nation, so we have to be able to be able to operate across a spectrum of conflict, including higher end missions."

A key driver of the change has been with regard to the ISR enablement of the fleet. They are focused increasingly on the left side of the kill chain, and leveraging ISR assets to be able to do so. In the kill chain focus, the priority emphasis has been upon target and engage with a priority training focus on targeting. "Now we need to focus much more on the find, fix and track functions. And we need to pay more attention on working with ISR assets to work the left side of the kill chain, and we have altered the syllabus to enable training to work the left side of the kill chain more effectively."

This is a shift from a kill chain to a kill web focus. In a kill web focus, the ISR assets which will help determine how the force package is formed, shaped and executes may or may not be organic parts of a pre-defined task force. The visit to Resolute Hunter in November 2020 highlighted how significant the shift is as the ISR assets were reworking their roles as collecting and delivering information to a decision maker in the battlespace to becoming integrated fusion centers able to deliver a decision or a decision recommendation or suggestion into the battlespace.

In terms of training, the syllabus emphasizes a couple of core changes. First, is the clear focus on mission command. "We take the mission commanders and challenge them to think through how various assets could be used in an ISR enabled strike package? How will they use the range of capabilities available? How can I as a strike commander take advantage of the sensors on a P-8? How do I ensure that I am getting the kind of information from a platform at the time I need it to execute my mission?"

As he explained the shift, the goal of the new syllabus is to address the paradigm shift with regard to ISR integrability into the strike force. The syllabus is designed to be flexible enough to bring in a variety of assets to empower the mission commander and his strike force.

And it is very clear that the shift in training, which CDR Papaioanu described, is part of a broader change in the training function. Training in the new syllabus is highly interactive with real world evolution of combat capabilities and operations. This generates a continuous learning cycle for training from ops to training to development and back to ops.

The Role of the Fighter in the Kill Web

May 31, 2020

With the developing relationship between sensors and shooters in the maritime kill web, what is the evolving role of the fighter? The CO of TOPGUN, CDR Tim Myers highlighted in an interview how he compared and contrasted his experience during his previous tour at TOPGUN, in 2006 through 2009, to his current tenure as CO. In terms of continuity, he underscored that TOPGUN has always been staffed by innovative warfighters, whose experience in the fleet has meant that the organization's work on innovation of operational tactics has had a significant influence throughout the Navy writ large. A key difference between his time during his earlier tour and now is that NAWDC has become much more engaged than its predecessor organization in working on warfighting requirements. From his perspective, incorporating experience from warfighters on the tactical cutting edge is key to ensuring the Navy is developing capabilities that will fold into future operations.

Another key difference is the increasing importance of integrated operations across the entire joint force, and, of course, within the Navy. He noted that TOPGUN has a close working relationship with the U.S. Marine Corps, with five USMC instructors currently on the TOPGUN staff. The interoperability with the USAF is significant as well, with naval aviation billets at the 422nd Fighter Squadron in Nellis and the 6th Fighter Squadron JSF Weapons School. These billets are both filled by former TOPGUN instructors, ensuring close alignment between USAF and USN tactics.

CDR Myers underscored the key synergies being worked among MAWTS-1, Nellis, and NAWDC. He noted that with all three services flying the same combat fighter (in three variants of the Joint Strike Fighter with 80 percent commonality), they are improving their understanding of how to work jointly in the new strategic environment. And the joint cooperation leads to enhanced cross learning. For example, he noted that USAF experience in Integrated Air Defense System (IADS), rollback, over land, and offensive counter-air is something that naval aviators are leveraging, whereas the USAF is leveraging the Navy's expertise in maritime strike operations.

He then discussed the USAF-led WEST-PAC exercise held in January 2020, which highlighted the evolution of USAF thinking. The exercise had the stated purpose of distributing airpower throughout the operational area and working integratability to shape the desired combat effect, but it also demonstrated a USAF focus on working maritime strike with joint partners.

Clearly, the F-35 has now arrived with full force at TOPGUN, who graduated their first Joint Strike Fighter Class in April, bringing an increased focus on fourth- and fifth-generation combined tactics, which has allowed them to maximize the strengths and minimize the weaknesses of both the F/A-18E/F and F-35. For example, NAWDC has been able to leverage fifth-generation sensor fusion and target identification capabilities, contributions to kill web management, and enhanced survivability inside of certain weapons engagement zones while also taking advantage of the unconstrained form factors, greater weapons payload capabilities, and flexibility that come with a mature and evolved fourth-generation platform.

TOPGUN, as a component of NAWDC, is uniquely positioned to tackle integration both within a Carrier Strike Group as well ensure integratability within the joint force. NAWDC hosts the type weapons schools for the F/A-18E/F Super Hornet and F-35 Lightening II (TOPGUN), E/A-18G Growler (HAVOC), E-2C/D Hawkeye (CAEWWS), MH-60R/S Sea Hawk (SEAWOLF), and MISR staff officers, all under one roof.

The organization is also responsible for the integrated training and certification of every Carrier Air Wing prior to deployment. Bringing the sweep of virtually every key element of an aviation kill web together on the NAWDC range complex, they can examine this evolving synergistic fighter capability and rapidly work through how integratability is optimized with other elements of the sensor and strike force. By generating a fused picture, distributed strike can be delivered throughout a kill web concept of operations.

In discussions with the head of the Navy's Maritime Patrol Enterprise, Rear Admiral Garvin, he underscored that the Navy was not going through iterative, but rather a more dramatic, step change. CDR Myers concurred. For CDR Myers what the kill web was highlighting was a strategic opportunity: "How do you use information to distribute the coordination of fires to a point where you can accomplish fires more rapidly? Instead of fusing all of this information into a central hub and then distributing that information from some coordinated command level, the focus becomes finding ways to autonomously push all the most relevant information so that the warfighting assets at the tactical edge, with a comprehensive understanding of commander's intent, can take mission command to the point of execution."

The answer to the question posed at the outset of this chapter: Fighters comprise a force package at the tip of the spear for the kill web, combining advanced sensor packages with inherent survivability with the battle space awareness necessary to bring effective fires to bear.

With the introduction of the F-35 as a multidomain flying combat system, and in some ways with the evolving integration of the fighter force into a synergistic sensor-shooter lead element via fourth- and fifth-generation as a key enabler of the kill web itself, naval aviation demonstrates a promising way to leverage the strengths of its diverse platforms to shape the battlespace.

The Perspective from HAVOC

May 12, 2020

With the strategic shift from the land wars to engaging in higher end conflict situations with peer competitors, electronic warfare and its role is changing as well. CDR Brett Stevenson, the Commander of HAVOC, highlighted how HAVOC was addressing the changing combat environment and how the focus on force integration was a key driver in shaping a way ahead.

The first takeaway from the discussion with CDR Stevenson would start right there—it is about full spectrum of warfare, not just the high-end fight. Being able to operate within and to dominate the electromagnetic spectrum is not a nice to have capability but is becoming a core requirement for effective engagement in conflict scenarios across the spectrum of warfare.

The second takeaway is that HAVOC is not focused on the management of a single exquisite platform per se, but upon how that platform operates in the joint force with other joint or coalition force assets to deliver the broad non-kinetic effect required.

In a core mission area, suppression of enemy air defenses, HAVOC is working closely with the USAF Weapons School at Nellis in shaping a variety of capabilities, including but not limited to F-35, Compass Call, space-based assets, and cyber-war assets to deliver the best air suppression capability possible. They along with the USAF are looking holistically at the integrated air defense system.

Within their domain, they are working a kill web approach to generate a synergy of effects enabling the force to take down air defense systems in a much more effective and efficient manner than if it was all about the Growler. In this case, it is about sensors and shooters working together through a non-kinetic kill web. When the CNO put out his FY21 Unfunded Priorities List (which includes next-generation jammer), it is interesting to note is that he equated NGJ and EW with increased lethality for the force. Integrating such capability into the overall strike mission is a virtual redefinition of what lethal strike actually means in a kill web approach.

A third takeaway is that all the hard work being done between HAVOC and Nellis is not just about honing current operational capabilities. It is in part, shaping how to leverage the sensors and capabilities inherent in Growler, which can be used within both kinetic and non-kinetic kill webs. It is also about shaping domain knowledge informing modernization approaches to the kill web EW capability as well.

This would mean it is not just about upgrading a particular platform but looking at the integrated effect and sorting through where major effects could be had by modernize particular tool sets which might be found on different platforms, rather than having to be resident on a particular platform. Not everyone needs to play quarterback.

The fourth takeaway is that HAVOC is preparing for the coming of the next-generation jammer pod on the Growler in the relative short term. Next-Gen jammer is the most significant leap in Navy EW since the introduction of Growler. Next-Gen jammers will bring a significant increase in both power and capacity to the Growler.

And that preparation process is not simply about HAVOC watching briefings. It is about being engaged in the test process as well. HAVOC is fully embedded within the NGJ test community and their industry partners. They are engaged in creating and validating tactics and initial employment options which means that when NGJ comes to the force, the learning curve to operational use will be significantly shortened.

One of NAWDC's main lines of effort is in creating, validating, and ultimately teaching advanced TTPs, and at no time is this effort more critical than when new capabilities are first introduced. Their role is to shape the way the force will employ these new technologies so that Carrier Air Wings can train to these standards, come to Air Wing Fallon to prove them on the range, then be ready to consistently and reliably deliver those capabilities in combat. This is why HAVOC has been involved in the development of NGJ from the start, and will see it through to fleet introduction and beyond.

The fifth takeaway is that preparation by HAVOC for NGJ is not simply about a particular technology. The HAVOC team is looking beyond their currently defined capabilities to figuring out what technologies are needed and how they would employ those to their benefit in a high-end fight.

The sixth takeaway is one which is true of most of the current training ranges. They were set up for legacy adversarial warfare, then adjusted to the global war on terror, and now back to the past, or adversarial warfare, but now in a different technological era. In the case of NAWDC, the EW ranges were conceived in the 1970s and the 1980s as a place where the carrier air-wing could conduct strike warfare training against an air defense system that replicated the capabilities and tactics of the Soviet Union.

There is clearly a challenge to ensure that the NAWDC range is resourced and equipped with the right training systems that will prepare carrier air-wings to be successful in the high-end fight and to do so within the context of rapidly changing technologies on BOTH the red and blue sides.

And clearly, when it comes to EW, training is always going to be challenging because of the question of dealing with frequency restrictions. Frequency utilization is definitely a challenge that's inherent in operating and training for electronic warfare. This enhances the importance of the Australians joining the Growler community and building relevant test ranges in Australia as well. This also highlights the importance of live virtual constructive training in this domain as well as cross-linking capabilities in this non-lethal domain with the broader strike force.

The seventh takeaway is the coming of Growler Block II. The next iteration of the aircraft will provide additional sensor enhancements which will expand battle space awareness to the networked force. And with the evolving capabilities of software upgradeability, there is a clear prospect of proliferating EW capabilities as well within the networked force. The expanded presence of remote assets will play a role as well in expanding the reach of EW capabilities woven into the kill web as well.

An eighth takeaway is about allies and the Growler. We did discuss the potential German acquisition of the Growler as well. The Germans are long standing partners with the U.S. Navy as well in EW. The CDR noted that there is a long-standing exchange officer program with the Luftwaffe at VAQ-129, the Growler training squadron. This means that UK and German legacy EW training via Tornado plus the Australians would add up to an EW coalition being trained in the evolving and developing twenty-first-century approach to EW.

And the final takeaway is one of the most important from the discussion, namely, the addition of non-kinetic targeteers to the air wing. Certainly, kinetic targeteers have been part of the air wing for a long time, but with the growing importance of the non-kinetic domain and its integration into kill web operations, there is a growing need for targeting knowledge in the non-kinetic domain.

Growler intelligence officers are fully integrated in the mission planning, execution and debriefing process along with the Growler operators. The non-kinetic targeteers comprise both Growler Squadron Intel Officers, and their enlisted Intelligence Specialists and Cryptological Technicians. These subject matter experts integrate into the broader Carrier Air Wing intel team, applying their non-kinetic targteteering expertise to aid in mission planning and to inform the efforts of intel collection managers for the entire Carrier Strike Group.

What that then provides is a team able to analyze an air defense problem and determine where the Growler capabilities would fit most effectively in the Suppression of Enemy Air Defense (SEAD) mission. This means as well that they will need to know what the other platforms relevant to a SEAD mission could contribute to sort through the most effective division of labor in executing the joint mission.

This means as well these officers can help support not only the Growlers but the entire air-wing to understand the evolving threat which means that the understanding of threat envelope is being continuously maintained and refreshed. In other words, the air wing has on board officers who can inform the operational community about the changing nature of the threat being experienced in ongoing operations.

More generally, there is a fourteen-week course at HAVOC, that is a distinct training process that produces "Growler Intelligence Officers," which are Intel "patch-wearers" similar to Growler Tactics Instructors (GTI), or TOPGUN graduates. These highly specialized Intel Officers will either remain on the NAWDC staff, serve at the Electronic Attack Weapons School in Whidbey Island, or other billets where specialized knowledge of non-kinetic effects is desired. They are distinct from the intel team on a Carrier Air Wing staff.

In short, HAVOC is working within the Navy, the joint force, and the coalition a way ahead with regard to kinetic and non-kinetic kill web capabilities. Given the growing potential of such systems within the evolving battlespace, there will be no end of opportunities and challenges for this part of Naval Aviation.

Electronic Warfare in the High-End Fight

October 6, 2020

During a July 2020 visit to NAWDC, the discussion with now Captain Brett Stevenson continued with the focus being upon the return of EW, the changing nature of EW, the shaping of Growler Block II, and the challenge of training for EW in the high-end fight.

The first is basic one: electronic warfare for the fleet was largely in support of the land wars, not a core competence practiced as part of the maritime fight. As Captain Stevenson put it: "In the post-cold war environment we have allowed ourselves to not focus so much on EW. The average strike group commander did not have to worry about this threat. But we have rediscovered that hiding the strike group as you transit is a key part of the maritime battle. We are having to relearn skill sets."

The second is that it is really about not just relearning but new learning patterns as well. The shift is from platform-specific EW delivery to working networks of sensors, to shape the kind of combat effect one would want. According to Captain Stevenson: "We envision networks of sensors that will be contributing to the common operating picture. That means quicker, more accurate geo locations with sensors contributing to the picture."

The third is the coming of Growler BLOCK 2. What Captain Stevenson highlighted was not so much an aircraft designed to be an exquisite platform to do EW as a platform evolving to become a quarterback within the EW combat environment. "What is driving Block II is a reassessment of capabilities to enhance our ability to prevail in the battlespace and overcome gaps that we currently have. Growler Block 2 will be a complete redesign of the crew-vehicle interface. We are looking now at questions such as follows: What processes should be automated? We are looking for ways to allow the crew to focus on the higher-level decision-making. How are data presented so that it is easier to make better decisions? We are focused on ways to ensure that the right data is presented to the crew at the right time."

"The new sensors are really the fundamental change that brings new capabilities. The Crew Vehicle Interface (CVI) makes the operator more efficient at employing those capabilities. We need to go beyond the aircraft and leverage connectivity to understand what other sensor nodes can provide. There will be more focus on being EW battle manager rather than being a specialized EW aircraft doing the job by ourselves."

In effect, Growler Block II is a reimaging of the aircraft and how it fits into the extended battlespace. Reimaging what an EW mothership looks like, MISR officers will contribute as well by tapping into national technical means as well to input to the EW management process. This is where multidomain becomes a credible combat capability in the EW warfare area.

But the fourth area is a very challenging one. How do you train to deliver EW capability in a rapidly changing technological and combat environment? Simply mastering the Growler as a combat platform is clearly not enough. And this is true not just because of the shift to a kill web enabling and delivery system for electronic warfare; it is also about the nature of the signals one is training against. Historically, one would work with a library of threats and train to operate against those threats guided by the intelligence library.

As Captain Stevenson put it: "We need to be able to predict how systems will respond to our capabilities and countermeasures; and we need to shape cognitive EW systems that enable us to look at how a signal behaves in response to certain stimuli and then be able to adapt and have an effective response." How do you train to this? And even more significant, as one trains, one is also guiding the question of the further development of the systems in the EW offensive and defensive combat force as well.

The range issue is an important one as well. "There are capabilities we would like to train to—being mindful of spectrum constraints, operational security, etc.—that are difficult on a range. How do we balance a high-fidelity live-flight experience on a training range with the benefits of training in a connected simulator environment?"

In short, in this critical combat area, innovations in training will be a key part of shaping an effective force going forward. But what innovations can be shaped to ensure this happens?

The Hawkeye/Stingray Cluster

May 6, 2020

In discussions in San Diego with Vice Admiral Miller, the Navy Air Boss, at the beginning of 2020, we focused on the dynamics of change within and beyond the carrier air wing. In that discussion, what was highlighted was a way to look at the shift from a legacy approach to the kill web approach, namely, the shift from the integrated to the integratable air wing. That discussion focused on the shift from integrating the air wing around relatively modest and sequential modernization efforts for the core platforms to a robust transformation process in which new assets enter the force and create a swirl of transformation opportunities, challenges, and pressures.

We discussed what might be called clusters of innovation, such as would be introduced as the MQ-25A Stingray comes onboard the carrier. In effect, the MQ-25 will be a stakeholder in the evolving C2/ISR capabilities empowering the entire combat force, part of what is really sixth-generation capabilities, namely, enhancing the power to distribute and integrate a force as well as to operate more effectively at the tactical edge. From this point of view, the MQ-25 will entail changes to the legacy air fleet, changes in the con-ops of the entire Carrier Air Wing (CVW) and trigger further changes with regard to how the C2/ISR dynamic shapes the evolution of the CVW and the joint force. The systems to be put onto the MQ-25 will be driven by overall changes in the C2/ISR force.

The cluster of innovation with the coming of the MQ-25A is being led by the transition from the legacy Hawkeye to the Aerial Refueling modified E-2D (AR) Advanced Hawkeye, which provides a game changing capability to a carrier air wing through advanced sensors and C2 networking capabilities, persistent presence, and greater operational reach.

That point was driven home in a discussion with CDR Christopher "Mullet" Hulitt, head of CAEWWS, the Navy's airborne command and control weapons school located at NAWDC. As the cluster evolves, the notion of a platform-centric functional delivery of airborne early warning and battle management shifts to a wider notion of providing support to the distributed integrated combat force which flies off of the carrier and adjacent capabilities working with the air maritime deployed kill web.

The first takeaway from that discussion was precisely the emergence of a different approach from the legacy Hawkeye to a new operational and training configuration. With the coming of the MQ-25A Stingray and emerging integrated sensor and command and control capabilities, the "Airborne Early Warning" community has transitioned its role and title to reflect emerging roles and functions within a maritime kill web, with an Airborne Command & Control and Logistics Wing under the leadership of a Commodore.

The second takeaway is that with the coming of the F-35 to the carrier wing, there is a broader shift in working diverse sensor networks to deliver the combat effect which extended reach sensor networks can empower. At Fallon, they are working the relationship between the F-35 and the E-2D and sorting through how to make optimal use of both air systems in the extended battlespace. Commander, Airborne Command & Control and Logistics Wing and Carrier Air Wing Two and are moving forward with a new initiative, the First Integrated Training Evolution (FITE), which will provide basic, tailored integrated training incorporating E-2D(AR) and F-35 paired with fourth-generation platforms. It is about deploying an extended trusted sensor network, which can be tapped through various wave forms, and then being able to shape how the decision-making arc can best deliver the desired combat effect.

The third takeaway is that the foundation is clearly being laid for the decade ahead for a fully operational maritime kill web. The strategic objective is to be able to operate extended reach, integratable, and interconnected sensor networks that provide the reach of the air wing beyond where physically its flies to deliver an extended reach combat effect.

The fourth takeaway is that the radar on the advanced Hawkeye is not in any way a traditional radar. The problem of terminology in discussing the new combat capabilities is certainly highlighted when discussing radars, built around modules which have a variety of combat capabilities built in, and in the case of the E-2D (AR), the traditional line between what airborne command & control, sensors, and electronic warfare systems do is clearly being subsumed into new integrative capabilities that can do more than the sum of the parts.

The fifth takeaway is that with the arrival of software upgradeable aircraft like the E-2D (AR), integrated with the MQ-25A, the entire process of evolving combat capabilities onboard an aircraft, and its ability to operate as an integratable of a kill web is changing significantly.

The goal is to get to the point where the core platforms are flexible enough to evolve software rapidly and interactively. And rather than having to ensure that each platform is maximized for what it can do with organic systems, the approach would be to determine which platforms with which capabilities can be a tasked for different functions and through integratability be able to contribute to a wider array of tasks as well.

For example, with the coming of the MQ-25A working with the E-2D (AR), evolving the sensor loadout on the MQ-25A along with reach back to Triton can not only allow the E-2D (AR) to do core functions differently but also adjust how it can provide support for evolving C2 tasking as well. Rather than following a classic AWACS like target identification and strike tasking function, the manned aircraft function will be to support the dynamic force packaging function in the extended battlespace. With regard to the E-2D (AR), the Navy is designing interfaces to manage the airborne MQ-25A.

And with the advanced Hawkeye, there is a shift to operating two aircraft at the same time, replicating to some extent the four-ship formation approach of an F-35 whereby the four ships operate as one combat brain within the airspace in which they are operating. This is a shift from the legacy Hawkeye where one aircraft operated off of the carrier to a seamless integration of a two-ship formation of Advanced Hawkeyes.

The sixth takeaway is with the coming of the subsurface and surface weapons schools as participants in NAWDC, the focus of operations for the E-2D(AR)/MQ-25A Stingray cluster will be upon 360-degree domain knowledge and combat support to leverage assets throughout the maritime kill web.

The seventh takeaway is that the process of change we saw when visiting NAWDC a few years ago is accelerating. What we saw then was shaping a way ahead to open the aperture of training to prepare for the coming of the F-35 and the focus on continuous development associated with the integratable air wing. In the case of CAEWWS, they will shortly have direct access to an integrated test configured aircraft. This allows CAEWWS to operate an aircraft which is a baseline above the capability of what Navy operational test squadrons are flying.

This is especially crucial in an era of software block upgradeable aircraft. NAWDC is in a position to release their recommendations concurrent with initial operational capability of a particular aircraft. This means that when a new capability rolls out, they are able concurrently to provide vetted employment recommendations from NAWDC and its weapon school partners.

In short, the transition from core function platforms to working as enablers and nodes in a kill web is underway at NAWDC. And the coming of the Advanced Hawkeye along with the Stingray in the same innovation cluster is a case in point.

With regard to the arrival of the air refuelable advanced Hawkeye, an interview with CDR Neil Fletcher, CO of VAW 121, on October 21, 2020, highlighted how the air refuelable aspect of an advanced Hawkeye reinforced the changes discussed by CDR Christopher Hulitt. The advanced Hawkeye has joined the fleet as the fleet is undergoing significant change to focus on the high-end fight, and to deliver capabilities to an evolving process of integratability. With the extended range air refueling brings to the Advanced Hawkeye plus the coming of the MQ-25 to the large deck carrier to do that air-refueling mission, the contribution of the aircraft will be enhanced for the fleet operating in the extended battlespace.

CDR Fletcher highlighted the importance of this new capability for the aircraft. "We should receive our first AR aircraft shortly. We will be the second squadron to complete the AR transition. By next year we will be fully transitioned as an AR squadron.

"This will give us more time on station and increase our range. We have always been focused on the carrier strike group, but throughout my career we have also supported the joint fight, so this capability will enhance our contribution. We've always been an integratable asset, but AR will make us just that much more capable as we extend our on-station time."

With the new advanced Hawkeye there is more capability in the aircraft to integrate with the mission. He noted that even though the aircraft looks much like its predecessor, "the advancements in technology with the digital generation, allows us to pack a lot more capability within the aircraft and also allows us to work differently in the battlespace."

There has been an important branding change which reflects the shift as well. They are now an airborne command and control squadron, rather than being labelled an airborne early warning squadron. As CDR Fletcher put it: "That branding change is purposeful; it is an evolution incorporating technological advances which enable us to be more interconnected, and more integratable. Much like we are more interconnected through the internet, which has changed all of our lives, its doing the same for naval aviation and the military."

One can accept the evolution point, but integratability is posing a significant shift as well. Certainly, for the weapons officers in the back of the aircraft, the challenge now is to manage a much wider range of data sources to shape C2 information flows as well. As the U.S. Navy evolves its concepts of operations to distributed maritime operations, certainly the capabilities in AR advanced Hawkeye will become even more important for the air wing of the future, or the integratable air wing.

The Role of Rotary Wing Platforms

May 1, 2020

In an April 2020 discussion with CDR Jeremy "Shed" Clark, Senior Leader at the Naval Rotary Wing Weapons School (SEAWOLF) at NAWDC, the role of rotary wing platforms in the evolving air wing was the focus of attention. The Seawolf School focuses on Romeo, Sierra, and Fire Scout training, with Romeo being the sensor rich ASW/SUW/EW and related tasked focus helicopters onboard the Navy's large deck carriers.

There is a shift under way from focusing largely on a targeted task for carrier defense and upon how the organic capabilities on the Romeo and Sierra could play their task most effectively to one where the focus is on broadening the sensor and strike partners of these platforms that can contribute to carrier strike and defense.

The first point which emerged from the discussion was that the aperture of considering the role of all rotary wing assets expands significantly as one shifts from a legacy carrier strike operation focus to broader support to a distributed maritime force. Due to the nature of where helicopters deploy this means that the sensors onboard these platforms can see their reach significantly expanded by being able to integrate with other sensors in the battlespace. Rather than being platform focused, the shift is to empower the Romeo/Sierra/Fire Scout and their reach with an expanded sensor network. This sensor network will be found both onboard each helicopter as well as with other aircraft onboard the carrier, but more broadly into the interactive allied working capabilities in the expanded battlespace.

The second point is that new assets coming onboard the carrier are going to be looked at from the outset in terms of what they can contribute to the sensor network and decision-making capabilities of the strike force. For example, the Romeo community is already looking at how having sensors onboard the MQ-25 can expand the reach and range of what the Romeo's onboard sensors can accomplish for the maritime distributed force.

It is also the case that as sensor demands currently made on the Romeo can be shifted elsewhere, the Romeo can refocus its task priorities and enhance its contributions to broader mission sets such as ASW and to focus on contributing capabilities that other platforms within the strike group are not prioritized to perform.

The third point is that the new generation of Navy operators are clearly thinking in kill web terms—they are not focused simply on what their platform can do based on how they were trained, but how they can work in the broader battlespace to deliver the desired effects working closely with partners in the sensor, decision-making, and strike web. He argued that this meant that NAWDC is looking at how to change the entire dynamic of the strike group with such an approach.

The fourth point is that with the distributed sensor network being built, manned helicopters can reduce the amount of time they need to be airborne to provide a core sensor set of tasks. The so-called unmanned revolution is ultimately about expanding the sensor network and allowing the manned operators within that network to operate more efficiently and more effectively; it is not primarily about replacing them in the battlespace.

The fifth point is that the kill web learning curve has a major impact on thinking about acquisition. Rather than focusing on the systems proprietary to a specific task-oriented platform, the focus is shifting toward integratability: What system can one tap onboard my platform via integratability with other combat assets, and what systems does one have onboard which provide a specific capability which the kill force needs to be able to leverage to enhance combat effectiveness?

The sixth point we discussed was the repurposing of the Fire Scout unmanned system. Originally, this was platform tasked, namely, to support the littoral combat ship. But with the new approach of utilizing all assets within a kill web, the question is how the helicopters working with Fire Scout can add the fleet needed capabilities, and where might the Fire Scout operate from within the fleet to gain maximum impact? This a significant shift and part of the dynamics of change unfolding at NAWDC. And CDR Clark highlighted that his team is working on ways to deliver some EW capability via Fire Scout integration with assets onboard the Growler EW aircraft.

In short, the shift is dramatic. Historically, training was done in stove pipes. One would train to be the best operator you could be on that platform. Now, that is not enough; obviously critical but the foundation for working a different way. The focus is upon working in a kill web and cross-linking capabilities within a distributed integrated force.

Rotary Wing Innovation

With the shift from the primacy of the land wars to a return to Blue Water operations, the capabilities of the systems onboard the Romeo helicopter have been given much more prominence. Part of it is due to the work with Fire Scout for the S-60 community working through ways ahead for manned-unmanned teaming, which is an increasingly important aspect for shaping the way ahead. And part of this effort is due to the enhanced emphasis on shaping a wide range of ISR-capabilities to inform combat operations. Indeed, the Romeo was a participant in the Resolute Hunter exercise in November 2020 which highlights its ISR role as the whole role of ISR shifts in the forging the kill web approach.

In an interview conducted at NAWDC in July 2020, CDR Jeremy "Shed" Clark, CO of the Naval Rotary Wing Weapons School (SEAWOLF) at NAWDC noted: "The new generation of Navy operators are clearly thinking in kill web terms—they are not focused simply on what their platform can do based on how they were trained, but how they can work in the broader battlespace to deliver the desired effects working closely with partners in the sensor, decision-making, and strike web. He argued that this meant that

NAWDC is looking at how to change the entire dynamic of the strike group with such an approach."

One role discussed was how Romeo was working with Growler to deliver electronic warfare capabilities to the fleet. When the fleet transits narrower areas, the Romeo is working EW functions for the fleet. And to do so more effectively in the future, how should payloads be shared with unmanned systems, like the Fire Scout. And because they are already operating Fire Scout, it is not simply an abstract discussion, but can be translate into how the Firescout can work differently with the S-60s.

CDR Clark noted that the Seahawk community was increasingly engaged in the expanded ISR for the fleet. He noted that after officers come through the Seahawk program, they now spend time at MISR to focus on the ISR part of what the Romeo provides. They are focused on ways to use their systems in an integrated ISR environment. But he cautioned: "We are not training to our broader community." But he sees the MISR engagement as a way to shape that broader community focus. I did note that during my visit of the new building to host integrated simulators, there was no planned Romeo simulator in the building. He added: "We are currently working on a white paper on why such an acquisition is necessary and what capability the Romeo will bring to the integrability effort."

CDR Clark highlights the importance of identifying capability gaps and then looking at the operational platforms in terms of targeted modernization strategies. "We need to look at the gaps in the mission sets, and then consider the applicable platforms whose upgrades could close those gaps most expeditiously and cost effectively. We should look for the lowest cost solutions on a particular platform, rather than looking to upgrade the entire force. And such gaps could well be met by changes in USMC or USAF platforms, not just with regard to U.S. Navy platforms."

Operating as a kill web has clear implications for shaping modernization approaches for the platforms operating as an integrated force.

The Impact of MISR

July 31, 2020

In a January 2020 visit with VADM Miller in North Island, San Diego, the Vice Admiral highlighted the importance of the coming of MISR to the fleet. MISR officers are trained as ISR subject matter experts to operate at the fleet or CSG level and to work the sensor fusion for the integratable CVW. And it is at NAWDC, where the MISR officers are being shaped and trained.

CDR Pete "Two Times" Salvaggio is the Maritime ISR (MISR) Weapons School, Department Head (DH), and MISR & EP-3E Weapons and Tactics Instructor (WTI). The career of this officer spans the period prior to MISR, the creation of MISR and the maturation of the MISR and Minotaur initiatives, which are laying down the foundation for creating the sixth-generation force alluded to earlier in this book (page 56).

What CDR Salvaggio described in an interview in the Spring 2020 was a very creative and interactive process in which the Navy has been engaged with the other services and coalition partners in both reshaping and rethinking how the force operates and can operate going forward with the C2/ISR revolution underway.

He was trained as an EP-3 operator, and when he worked for then Captain Garvin who at the time was CPRW-10, the goal was to cross-link what EP-3s could do with the rest of the MPRF, which at the time included P-3s, BAMS-D RQ-4s, and Tactical Operations Centers (TOCs), to prepare the grounds for the coming of the P-8/Triton dyad. This initiative was combined with experiences in the land wars of Iraq and Afghanistan to lay the foundation for MISR.

What "Two Times" described was his experience in the Middle East working with the CENTAF Combined Air Operations Center (CAOC) as part of the USMC's third MEF operations in RC-South West as the EP-3E Detachment Officer in Charge (OIC). Lessons from those operations on how the Marines were dynamically integrating ISR feeds into the ground maneuver element set the initial foundation. With an ISR officer on the ground responsible for shaping the knowledge base for informing ground maneuver, it was obvious to "Two Times" and his senior officers that the Navy needed just such an approach in the years to come.

MISR prides itself in being both platform and sensor agnostic, along with employing an effects-based tasking and tactics approach that allows for shaping the ISR domain knowledge which a task force or fleet needs to be fully combat effective. What is most impressive is that CDR Salvaggio has been present at the creation and is a key part of shaping the way ahead in a time of significant change in what the fleet is being asked to do in both a joint and coalition operational environment.

And NAWDC clearly reflects and embodies this change. Over the past six years, NAWDC has gone from traditional CSG integration, to embedding the surface and subsurface weapons schools, to evolving a new approach to working the platform training side of NAWDC to embrace the shift to the integratable air wing, to standing up two new weapons schools which are kill web oriented, not platform oriented. The first school was highlighted in an interview with CDR Joseph Fraser, head of the Information Warfare Directorate, which has been designated the executive agent for targeting for the USN. The second school is the MISR weapons school. And to be clear, these are not simply layering on top of platform training schools; they are part of the cross-training which goes on within NAWDC.

But not just NAWDC, for working with the USAF and the USMC, as well as with the U.S.'s closest coalition partners, is crucial for shaping a way ahead. CDR Salvaggio underscored that one of his responsibilities at NAWDC is working the only ISR exercise conducted in the United States, one which includes those allies. With COVID-19 limitations, the November 2020 version of Resolute Hunter did not include allies, but did include the Marines and the USAF in shaping the MISR focused ISR led force empowerment approach.

Working the Left Side of the Kill Chain

The importance of MISR cannot be understated. As Vice Admiral Miller, the Navy's Air Boss has put it: "The next war will be won or lost by the purple shirts. You need to take MISR seriously, because the next fight is an ISR-led and enabled fight."

During the visit to NAWDC in July 2020, the discussion of MISR with the Department head, CDR Pete "Two Times" Salvaggio continued as well as having lunch with students in the course.

What is entailed in "Two Times" perspective is a cultural shift. "We need a paradigm shift: The Navy needs to focus on the left side of the kill chain." The kill chain is described as find, fix, target, engage, and assess. Kill chain is to find, fix, track, target, engage, and assess. For the USN, the weight of effort has been upon target and engage. As "Two Times" puts it "But if you cannot find, fix or track something, you never get to target."

There is another challenge as well: in a crisis, knowing what to hit and what to avoid is crucial to crisis management. This clearly requires the kind of ISR management skills to inform the appropriate decision makers as well.

The ISR piece is particularly challenging as one operates across a multi-domain battlespace to be able to identify the best ISR information, even it is not provided by the ISR assets within your organic task force. And the training side of this is very challenging. That challenge might be put this way: How does one build the skills in the Navy to do what you want to do with regard to managed ISR data and deliver it in the correct but timely manner and how to get the command level to understand the absolute centrality of having such skill sets?

"Two Times" identified a number of key parameters of change with the coming of MISR. "We are finally breaking the old mindset; it is only now that the department heads at NAWDC are embracing the new role for ISR in the fight. We are a unique organization at NAWDC for we do not own a platform. And the MISR school has both officers and enlisted in the team. We are not all aviators; we have intel specialists, we have cryptographers, pilots, crewmen, etc.

"Aviators follow a more rapid pace of actions by the mere nature of how fast the aircraft we are in physically move; non-aviators do not have the same pace of working rapidly within chaos. Our goal at MISR is to be comfortable to work in chaos."

Another part of the shift is to get recognition that ISR does not SUPPORT the force; it is an essential element of the combat capability for the force to be able to operate effectively or to lead the force. The kill web approach is about breaking the practice of correlating specific sensors with specific weapons; it is about shaping a much broader understanding of how to work sensor networks to deliver the outcome one is seeking.

"Two Times" argued that the training within NAWDC to train MISR officers is not bad, but the big challenge is to work to break down habitual operational patterns of senior commanders, who really are not focused on how the ISR revolution is changing warfighting. How to do a better job of linking up warfare training outside of NAWDC with the fleet?

They have deployed MISR officers on five CSGs to date; and the reaction of the senior officers is that they would never deploy again without this skill set. But it has taken two to three months during the deployment to get senior officers to gain appreciation of what a MISR officer can bring to the fight.

The kill web perspective is founded on a core combat platform or combat group understanding what adjacent forces, whether Navy, joint U.S. or coalition, can be leveraged for enhanced reach and combat effectiveness. The traditional CSG model focuses on its organic capabilities, and the skills are honed to get complete combat value from the integrated air wing working with the other elements of the carrier task force.

The kill web model is different. The CSG is operating in the extended battlespace. One is able to deliver multiple functionalities from the CSG, but the focus then is upon contribution to the extended fleet or combat force, but not just in terms of what a tightly integrated CSG can provide. This means that it is important to understand what the assets outside of the CSG can bring to the fight and, conversely, how carrier based assets can contribute more broadly to a distributed fleet or distributed joint or coalition forces as well.

And according to Two Times, this is one of the key foci of what MISR officers are addressing. "That is what we teach; we are an effects focused contributor; not a platform focused effort. There are not enough platforms to go around; not everyone is going to have their own P-8 but they may well need the kind of information which a P-8 like asset can provide. That is where the MISR approach comes in. You do not need to control the platform. Tell me what it is you need to know about, and we will reach out and find a way to get you that information. What critical pieces of information do you need to make the critical decision that you need to make. We will find a way to get you that information. And we work that entire process.

"We work for C2. Because this skill set has not existed in the Navy, there is a lot of ad hoc solutions to close the ISR gap. Under the MISR approach, the elements of the Navy operating force can leverage the broader ISR assets rather than having a platform lassoed by a command element to provide only for its own needs. The problem is that if that the command element is familiar with some platforms, but not others which could deliver the desired information."

In effect, the MISR officers are translators to the fleet of shaping requests for information to the kill web rather than to a specific Navy platform. "You can paint our uniforms into many colors. We are doing multi-domain ISR. We are building products for mission execution that get everyone on the same page."

There is another aspect of the coming of MISR to the fleet which could have a significant impact on operational capabilities beyond what "Two Times" discussed. And that flowed from conversations at lunch with the MISR course participants.

There is a clear opportunity to add passive sensing to platforms operating within the force. For example, the CMV-22Bs will fly to the fleet for the logistics function, but why not place passive sensors on the aircraft to scoop up ISR information which can be distributed to an appropriate functional area? For example, the Romeo, P-8 and Triton communities are working to shape more effective integration. Clearly, MISR officers will know that ISR dynamics within that functional area and might be the perfect players to suggest what passive sensing on the CMV-22B might best provide to that force package or to one of the elements within that package.

The coming of MISR is a key part of reshaping the force and building out a kill web foundation for the maritime force. But being knowledgeable about ISR assets throughout the joint and coalition force and being able to tap into those either at the level of CSG or numbered fleet levels will be a significant training challenge. And new ways will have to be found to meet those challenges for sure.

Dynamic Targeting

May 28, 2020

With the strategic shift from the land wars to the more fluid battlespace involving peer competitors engaged in full spectrum crisis management with the United States and its allies, one aspect of the change for military forces is how to use lethal force effectively. This comes down in part to how to target dynamically in a fluid political and military situation. And within the dynamics of management of escalation, how do I ensure that I have had the combat effect which provides an effective solution set?

From a strictly military point of view, the strategic shift is from deliberate to dynamic targeting. As one analyst has put the issue of the shift affecting the maritime domain: "Perhaps the most acute differences that the maritime theater will present are the target sets. Targets that can be categorized as deliberate will now be the exception to the rule. Relatively fixed land targets will yield to highly mobile maritime targets. Therefore, targets may be known but not fixed."[4]

How significant the shift is can be seen in a USAF explanation of the difference between deliberate and dynamic targeting. "Dynamic targeting complements the deliberate planning efforts, as part of an overall operation, but also poses some challenges in the execution of targets designated within

---

4   Lt. Commander Mitchell S. McCallister, "The Maritime Dynamic Targeting Gap," *Naval War College Review*, May 4, 2012.

the dynamic targeting process. Dynamic targets are identified too late, or not selected for action in time to be included in deliberate targeting."[5]

The assessment adds: "Dynamic targeting is a term that applies to all targeting that is prosecuted outside of a given day's preplanned air tasking order (ATO) targets (i.e., the unplanned and unanticipated targets). It represents the targeting portion of the "execution" phase of effects-based approach to operations (EBAO). It is essential for commanders and air operations center (AOC) personnel to keep effects-based principles and the JFC's objectives in mind during dynamic targeting and ATO execution.

"It is easy for those caught up in the daily battle rhythm to become too focused on tactical-level details, losing sight of objectives, desired effects, or other aspects of commander's intent. When this happens, execution can devolve into blind target servicing, unguided by strategy, with little or no anticipation of enemy actions."

But what if dynamic targeting becomes the norm and deliberate targeting the exception? With specific regard to the Pacific, the strategic shift could well generate a significant targeting shift. But how to train, plan, and execute a dynamic targeting approach?

That is a challenge being addressed by the NAWDC team, with CDR Joseph Fraser, head of the Information Warfare Directorate, which has been designated the executive agent for targeting for the USN.

There are a number of takeaways from that conversation. The first takeaway is simple enough: NAWDC is an integrated warfighting center, not simply the classic Top Gun venue. With officers from the various elements of Navy warfighting present within NAWDC, as well as enhanced engagement with the other services' warfighting centers, NAWDC makes perfect sense to work the 360-degree dynamic targeting solutions set for an integrated distributed force.

---

5   https://www.doctrine.af.mil/Portals/61/documents/Annex_3-60/3-60-D16-Target-Dynamic.pdf

Obviously, this is both challenging and a work in progress. But the core point is that Navy has laid the foundation within and at NAWDC to shape such a way ahead.

The second takeaway is that the new combat platforms coming into the force provide the information and data environment to work a dynamic targeting solution set. Notably, both the F-35 and the Advanced Hawkeye have come to the carrier wing since we were last at Fallon, but it is also the case that the data being generated by these aircraft are being worked across not only the fleet but also the joint combat force. Or put another way, the new platforms coming to the fleet are capable of enabling a kill web maritime force. The quality of the data that's coming off of these new platforms enables dynamic targeting.

The third takeaway is that with the reliance on a precision weapons stockpile, it is crucial to get best value out of that capability. It is not World War II weapons stockpiles at work; weapon effectiveness in terms of being able to identify and destroy targets that matter most need to be prioritized and dealt with in a combat situation.

The fourth takeaway is that within a cluttered maritime combat environment, target identification is always challenging, but if one wants to prioritize the most significant targets, clearly effective ISR with time urgent decision making against mobile targets is a key element for mission success.

The fifth takeaway is that by working a new model of dynamic weapons engagement now prior to the coming of directed energy weapons to the fleet, it will be possible to determine how to use these new technologies effectively by which platforms, in which situations and in which combat areas within the fluid and extended battlespace. This can also be true with regard to future precision weapons as well and can provide a guide for shaping a future weapons inventory. Which weapons would make a significant difference if added to the fleet to maximize dynamic targeting capabilities against which adversaries and in which situations?

The sixth takeaway is this is an area where expanded work with the other services is clearly crucial. But if the Pacific is taken as a baseline case, then the question of maritime targets, or targets that operate within that domain become crucial challenges to be dealt with. And these targeting challenges really have little to deal with the legacy targeting solution sets generated in the land wars, and, frankly, the lessons learned will have to be unlearned to some extent. What this means in blunt terms, is that the Navy plays a key role in this strategic targeting shift.

In short, we are talking about targeting solutions enabled by interactive webs, but not necessarily what passes for joint targeting. The maritime domain is very different from the land or air-space domain. While the U.S. Army and USAF can provide key capabilities to provide for dynamic targeting, the domain knowledge of the USN will be a central piece of the puzzle.

And much the same could be said with regard to the other domains, and what the role of the USN would be in a dynamic targeting solution set. Much like how words such as C2, ISR and training are being changed fundamentally in terms of their meaning with the building of a kill web integrated distributed force, the term joint also is changing, or will need to change if combat effectiveness is to be realized. There is a tendency to slip into the past twenty years of jointness that has been dominated by the US Army and the land wars. The Pacific is dramatically different.

Weapons, Crisis Management, and the High-End Fight

October 14, 2020

As the fleet re-works blue water maneuver warfare and expeditionary operations from the sea, a key element of the effort is shaping an effective weaponization approach and strategy. Doing so is a work in progress and a major challenge for the United States and its allies.

During discussions and visits to NAWDC, some elements which are crucial to shape an effective way ahead for the fleet, and the challenge as well of shaping the kind of training which will be needed to deliver the right combat effect at the right time were discussed.

The first point is pretty straightforward. The focus is upon how to shape fleet-wide targeting. This is part of the NAWDC-led effort to work TTPs for a force element, not just a single platform, or a platform operating off a single ship, such as Super Hornets working with an aircraft carrier.

The reason for this focus is rooted in a shift in how ISR is changing and how new options are becoming available for targeting, and as well how to do delivering targeting solutions. This is what is implied in the shift from the kill chain to the kill web. This was put particularly well by a senior RAAF commander in an interview I did with him in 2016. Because the Aussie Navy does not have an Air Force but relies on the RAAF to do the air part, they focus on integration at levels which in the United States requires two very large forces the USN and the USAF to work integrability.

"We need to be in the position where our maritime surface combatants are able to receive the information that we've got airborne in the RAAF assets. Once they've got that, they're going to actually be trying to be able to do something with it. That is the second level, namely, where they can integrate with the C2 and ISR flowing from our air fleet. But we need to get to the third level, where they too can provide information and weapons for us in the air domain.

"That is how you will turn a kill chain into a kill web. That's something that we want in our fifth-generation integrated force. And in a fifth-generation world, it's less about who is the trigger shooter, but actually making sure that everybody's contributing effectively to the right decisions made as soon as possible at the lowest possible level."[6]

A key element of the new approach is how platforms will interact with one another in distributed strike and defensive operations and enable cuing weapons across a task force.

The first point is rather significant—it is about how to leverage weapons capabilities across a task force and dynamically shaping an expanded capability and process for empowering third-party targeting.

6   Robbin Laird, "Shaping the Airpower Transition: The Perspective of 'Zed' Roberton, Commander Air Combat Group (RAAF), *Second Line of Defense* (April 6, 2016).

The second point is that there is a shift from a primary focus on deliberate targeting to dynamic targeting. There is a clear need to expand targeting domain knowledge to include both nonlethal and lethal effects. Because the kinds of nonlethal effects as discussed with CDR Stephenson, highlighted earlier, provide significant shaping functions in combat, nonlethal effects really need to factor into the entire sweep of how the strike function delivers combat effects.

CDR Fraser put it this way: "Nirvana for me is a fully integrated strike squadron capability that does both kinetic and non-kinetic missions to provide a range of options to the commander."

Part of the challenge is putting in place a cadre of officers with the kind of strike domain knowledge covering both lethal and nonlethal who are not attached to a particular carrier wing. This would allow for the strengthening of the cadre and the ability to deploy to the operational need, rather than the operating cycle of a particular air wing.

The third point flows from the second. How to shape dynamic targeting knowledge and training, notably in terms of the dynamics of change both in terms of ISR availability and the evolution of the weapons enterprise? How is one going to shape a training enterprise able to encompass fleet wide plus ISR (the MISR path) with knowledge of the various ways weapons which can be launched from air-sea-land locations to provide for the dynamic targeting required by the fleet?

The fourth point really would revolve around the weapons enterprise itself and how the fleet will be empowered by new ways to build out weapons arsenals and provide for adequate stockpiles for the force. That was the subject of conversation with Captain Edward Hill, the oldest Captain in the USN at sixty years of age. Because he goes back to the Cold War operating Navy, he can bring forward that experience to the return to the contested environment challenges facing the weapons enterprise.

Clearly, building adequate stockpiles of weapons is crucial. But also important is working a new weapons mix to ensure that one is not forced by necessity to rely on the most expensive weapons, and the ones that will almost always have a stockpiling issue, but to have a much more cost-effective weapons set of options.

As Captain Hill put it: "We need to get beyond golden bee-bee solution. We need to have a weapons barge come with the battle group that has an affordable weapons mix. We need $50,000 weapons; not just million-dollar weapons. We should have weapons to overwhelm an adversary with Joe's garage weapons and not having to use the golden bee-bees as the only option."

To get to this point raises a second aspect, namely, working out where one engages an adversary and what weapons mix one might need in that engagement area. With regard to the Pacific, as we address sea denial and sea control reaching out into the Sea Lines of Communications or SLOCS, what weapons mix do we need in which particular engagement zone? It is not going to be all about hypersonic weapons.

The third point is about the C2 side of weapons engagement. As Captain Hill put it: "How do we train to be prepared for C2 disruptions and conflict in a high-end fight." For a strike force, this is the critical element of ensuring an ability to leverage a distributed weapons capability, but to do so with effective determined targeting solutions with the kind of tactical or strategic effect one is seeking. This means that C2 enabling an integrated distributed it force is not only a weapon but also the foundational weapon enabling change in dynamic targeting for an innovative weapons enterprise.

One of the clearest expressions of the way ahead along these lines was an interview which I did in 2016 in Australia, with Rear Admiral Mayer, the commander of the Australian Fleet. This is how he characterized the C2 side of the weapons enterprise for an integrated but distributed force.

"The potential of each of the individual platforms in a network is such that we've actually got to preset the limits of the fight before we get to it. The decisions on what we'll do, how much we'll share, and what sovereign rights we will retain have to be preset into each one of the combat systems before you switch it on and join a network.

"There is no point designing a combat system capable of defeating supersonic threats and throttling it with a slow network or cumbersome C2 decision architecture. Achieving an effective network topology is so much more complex in a coalition context in which the potential for divergence is higher.

"The paradox is that a coalition network is much more likely a requirement than a national network, and yet what investment we do make is based on national systems first. If we don't achieve the open architecture design that enables the synergy of a networked coalition force, then the effectiveness of the coalition itself will be put at risk. The moment we insert excess command and hierarchical decision authority into the loop, we will slow down the lethality of the platforms in the network.

"Before we even get in the battlespace, we have to agree the decision rights and preset these decisions into the combat system and network design; the fight for a lethal effect starts at the policy level before we even engage in combat operations.

"The network and C2 rather than the platforms can become the critical vulnerability. This is why the decision-making process needs to be designed as much as the network or the platforms. If the C2 matrix slows the network, it will dumb down the platform and the capability of the system to deliver a full effect.

"The nature of the force we are shaping is analogous to a biological system in which the elements flourish based on their natural relationship within the environment. We have an opportunity to shape both the platforms and the network, but we will only achieve the flourishing ecosystem we seek if each harmonize with the other, and the overall effectiveness is considered on the health of the ecosystem overall.

"For example, an ASW network will leverage the potential of the individual constituent platforms and that in turn will determine the lethality of the system. A discordant network connection will, at the least, limit the overall force level effect of the network and at worst break the network down to discordant elements."

Clearly, a key part of the evolution is about shaping a weapons revolution whereby weapons can operate throughout the battlespace hosted by platforms that are empowered by networks tailored to the battlespace. And that revolution will have its proper impact only if the network and C2 dynamics discussed by Rear Admiral Mayer unfold in the national and coalition forces.

"The limiting factor now is not our platforms; it's the networks and C2 that hold the potential of those platforms down. When the individual platforms actually go into a fight, they're part of an interdependent system; the thing that will dumb down the system will be a network that is not tailored to leverage the potential of the elements, or a network that holds decision authority at a level that is a constraint on timely decision-making. The network will determine the lethality of our combined system."[7]

The strategic shift from the land wars highlights the growing role of dynamic targeting in a contested environment. And as new platforms and capabilities come into the force, they can be looked at in terms of how these new capabilities empower a kill web force, rather than simply fitting into the older kill chain approach.

For the USN at NAWDC, the next generation carrier, the *USS Ford* can be viewed from this prism. A recent visit to the *USS Ford* highlighted how indeed the next-generation carrier is best understood from the standpoint of being able to deploy an integratable air wing and empowering interactive maritime kill webs in the extended battlespace.[8]

---

7   Robbin Laird, "The Network as a Weapon System: The Perspective of Rear Admiral Mayer, Commander Australian Fleet," *Second Line of Defense* (September 10, 2016), https://sldinfo.com/2016/09/the-network-as-a-weapon-system-the-perspective-of-rear-admiral-mayer-commander-australian-fleet/

8   Robbin Laird, "The Coming of the USS Gerald R. Ford: October 2020 Report," *Defense.info* (October 2020), https://defense.info/highlight-of-the-week/the-coming-of-the-uss-gerald-r-ford-october-2020-report/.

Reshaping Combat Architecture and Training

October 9, 2020

With the shift from the land wars to rebuilding U.S. forces for contested operations with peer competitors, the role of training is changing significantly. There clearly was innovation during the land wars, but the geographical battlespace was well-known, and air and maritime power could operate with impunity in support of ground forces, whether for the maneuver force or counter-insurgency forces.

Those skill sets and concepts of operations reshaped U.S. military forces but in so doing created a generation that has not faced adversaries focusing on denying sea and airspace to those U.S. military forces. As Major James Everett, Head of the Assault Support Department at MAWTS-1 has put it:

"The vast majority of us grew up in a Fleet Marine Force that understood and constantly trained to fight the insurgencies that ripened in these uncertain environments. And we've become quite proficient at it. However, over the past fifteen years, threat of another Great Power Competition has grown quietly in the background.... Now, having been content to watch China's rise and its concurrent development and maturation of a modern military, we are faced with a force of devastating potential. This problem set is wildly different than anything that we, as planners and operators, have ever faced before."[9]

So how do you train in such a way that you are able to break old patterns and learn new ones? Or even more challenging, how do you shape what those new skill sets need to be?

Shaping a transition from the land wars to full spectrum crisis management is a very significant one, but that transition is enabled by the introduction of new platforms, technologies and approaches. There is much discussion of multi-domain warfare, but what is really happening with the

---

9   Major James Everett, "The Peer Fight is Coming: How do we prepare?" *Second Line of Defense* (September 18, 2020), https://sldinfo.com/2020/09/the-peer-fight-is-coming-how-do-we-prepare/.

current force, is leveraging new capabilities to allow for force packages or modules to work together in new ways. And this is built around a number of innovations in the ISR and C2 domains but does not require the entire force to operate as a multi-domain combat capability.

The combat architecture is evolving and being reshaped in operations, and in training. In fact, training, operations, and development are part of an interactive cycle whereby U.S. military forces are being reshaped in a dynamic and ongoing manner.

During my visit to NAWDC in July 2020, one clear indication of the change could be seen with the NAWDC's focus on hosting working groups to redesign the tactics, techniques and procedures, with the operators and for the operators. It is not just about learning the TTPs for the integrated air wing; it is about rethinking, reworking and training the maritime force to work in an integrated, distributed manner, to deliver the desired combat effect.

Put bluntly, this is about force operational redesign driven by the inputs from the fleet planners as well as key military training centers. What this approach highlights are the gaps which emerge as integrability is worked and recommendations with regard to acquisition of where best to fill those gaps. This is an open-ended process, not a closed loop.

During my July 2020 NAWDC visit, I had a chance to discuss this evolving approach with CDR Jeremy "Shed" Clark, Senior Leader at the Naval Rotary Wing Weapons School (SEAWOLF) at NAWDC, and with CDR Tim Myers, the CO of TOPGUN at NAWDC. The topic of the working group-led approach to redesign came into the discussion with CDR Clark after we finished our discussion on the Romeos' ASW mission sets. He argued that they needed to look at where improvements would most benefit the fleet, and then consider the applicable platforms whose upgrades could address those areas most expeditiously and cost effectively. The goal would be to look for the most advantageous solutions on a particular platform, rather than looking to upgrade the entire force. These solutions could well be provided via changes or upgrades to other (non-aviation) DoD platforms, identifying a need for a holistic approach.

CDR Clark argued that the USN's ASW community pursued something akin to this in the 1980's and 90's but moved away from the approach as ASW became of lesser significance. This meant that for the last decade plus, more stove piped views have prevailed.

But NAWDC is leading a new approach. According to CDR Clark, "We have set up a number of working groups to look at the broader mission areas and to rise to the challenge of establishing the larger TTPs for those mission areas. For example, we are looking at how we can accomplish defense of the fleet across the joint force, and then identifying any mission gaps we may have. Then the question is how would we close those gaps across our joint force?"

He noted that they are scheduling quarterly working groups, which include the USAF and USMC as well. While COVID-19 has complicated the schedule, the trajectory is clear. "If we are going to do a full maritime strike, what would that look like and who can contribute?" In the first quarter of this year, NAWDC hosted such a working group which lasted for two weeks and essentially was focused on functional TTPs vice platform centric TTPs. This was the first time NAWDC did this. Such a "training approach" raises key questions about how best to train to fleet wide TTPs based on joint capabilities. "This will open people's eyes to optimizing the acquisition process to fill critical needs."

The first working group was done largely within the Navy weapons schools but with clear intent to broaden the joint participation. In addition, fleet planners are being included as part of the broader effort. "The approach has been to bound the problem at NAWDC and then take the effort outside for wider fleet and joint force engagement."

I was able to continue this discussion with the CO of TOPGUN. He is also the action officer for the working groups. "We want to shape a process that could deliver a valuable product, rather than just having a set of meetings. We want products that are key parts of the rethinking process."

Now that they have demonstrated the proof of concept, they are focused on growing the effort. They are framing key questions which allow for interactive working on end-to-end con-ops. What is really being discussed is shaping a kill web-enabled force; one in which the area of interest by the assets currently engaged in combat can work together to deliver the kind of combat affects you want to achieve. A kill web is focused on combat effects, while a kill chain is focused on targeting as its primary outcome. A kill web is about creating a foundation to allow strike group commanders to think about how they employ their combat assets in conjunction with relevant joint or coalition assets, rather than just relying on what they organically own.

After we had the July 2020 discussion, the next working group met and focused on counter-air operations. defense. According to CDR Myers, "The working group included USAF fifth generation pilots, unmanned combat asset operators, suppression of air defense experts, DoD weapons subject matter experts, and Navy undersea warfare and SEAL officers."

CDR Myers noted: "We have shared the maritime strike concept of operations with the USAF as they are working on how to project power into the maritime domain. A lot of these TTPs translate nicely to USAF operations." The teams are working a very different approach to joint operations in the Pacific compared to joint practices used in the Middle East.

Their ultimate vision is to convene quarterly working groups that would focus on developing the right kind of methodology; maritime strike, counter IADS, full-spectrum defense of the fleet, then more classic air interdiction in more permissive environments. The classic Air Wing has developed lots of capital in this fourth one, but maritime strike, counter IADS and defense of the fleet required a significant rework, applying gap analysis to shape the way ahead.

CDR Meyers added: "The timeline for implementing these tactical changes is aggressive. To accelerate learning, we are providing these new CONOPS to the fleet and asking for feedback. Strike groups are executing our TTPs as a part of their work-up cycles, and we are immediately taking their lessons learned, what worked and what didn't, and folding them back into the process."

"Our CONOPS are written generically but can be applied to specific scenarios. We plan to take the counter-IADS product and have the working group apply it to some very specific operational plans. This will serve as an exemplar for the CONOPs, and hopefully provide constructive feedback to the operational planners."

"Several feedback mechanisms are in play; we receive feedback on our CONOPS from the Fleet, and as a result of our integrated training events; we provide feedback to the fleet operational planners, including asset allocation, missions and target sets, prioritized targeting lists – all of these feedback mechanisms are going through NAWDC. These functions are really not platform-centric and are happening across platforms; some platforms are optimized for specific aspects of the functions which need to be performed, and others for other aspects; and at certain periods of time, in the combat space."

This is a very different concept of training than what was inherited from the land wars - one designed to empower the combat force with innovation from within, rather than being designed in a briefing room and enforced by a hierarchical centralized command. In other words, the ops, training, and development cycle is being reworked, and with it the combat force incorporating those changes and driving further change. As a result, the kind of innovation required for escalation dominance and control is much more likely to be generated.

CHAPTER THREE:

JAX NAVY SHAPES A TRANSITION

Overview

The Maritime Patrol Reconnaissance Force (MPRF) is organized into two Patrol and Reconnaissance Wings at NAS Jacksonville, Florida, and NAS Whidbey Island, Washington including 14 Patrol and Reconnaissance squadrons, one Fleet Replacement Squadron (FRS) and over 45 subordinate commands. The MPRF is the Navy's premier provider for airborne ASW, Anti-Surface Warfare (ASuW), and maritime Intelligence, Surveillance, and Reconnaissance (ISR) operations.

Currently, the core platforms used by the MPRF are the P-8A and the MQ-4C. These platforms are not simply replacement platforms for the P-3 and EP-3. The change is as dramatic as the Marines going from the CH-46 to an Osprey which could only be described as a process of transformation rather than a transition from older to newer platforms.

These platforms, are a synergistic 'Family of Systems' empowering global MDA and the joint strike enterprise. Most importantly, while the P-8A is a capable engagement platform in its own right, the information generated by the P-8A/MQ-4C dyad empowers and enhances the organic ASW strike capability on the P-8. Moreover, the entirety of Department of Defenses' strike capability is enhanced against adversarial multi-domain forces.

Although these are U.S. Naval platforms, they are designed to connect with the larger C2/ISR infrastructure, changing the capabilities and operations of the entire U.S. and allied combat forces. These platforms provide significant SA for a task force and can operate in effect as combat clouds for a tailored task force operating across the spectrum of conflict. With the coming of Triton, a completely new approach is being shaped on how to operate, and leverage the data and systems onboard the manned and unmanned air systems joined at the hip, namely, the P-8 and the Triton.

There is an obvious return to the anti-submarine mission by the United States and allied navies with the growing capabilities of the twenty-first-century authoritarian powers. However, as adversary submarines evolve, and their impact on warfare becomes even more pronounced, ASW can no longer be considered as a narrow warfighting specialty. It is not simply about organic capabilities on the aircraft to conduct ASW. The P-3 flew alone and unafraid; the dyad is flying as part of a wider networked enterprise, and one which can be tailored to a threat, or an area of interest, and can operate as a combat cloud empowering a tailored force designed to achieve the desired combat effects.

The information generated by the "Family of Systems" can be used with the gray zone forces such as the USCG cutters or the new Australian Offshore Patrol Vessels. The P-8/Triton dyad is a key enabler of full spectrum crisis management operations, which requires the kind of force transformation which the P-8/Triton is a key part of delivering the United States and core allies.

A key consideration is the growing importance of what one might call "proactive ISR." It is crucial to study the operational environment and to map anomalies; this provides a powerful baseline from which to prepare future operations, which require force packages that can deliver the desired kinetic or non-kinetic effect.

Moreover, an unambiguous understanding of the environment, including patterns of life and timely recognition of changes in those patterns, serves to inform decision makers earlier and perhaps seek solutions short of kinetic. This is not about collecting more data for the intelligence community back in the United States; it is about generating operational domain knowledge that can be leveraged rapidly in a crisis and to shape the kind of C2 capabilities which are required in combat at the speed of light.

Success rests on a significant rework of C2 networks to allow a distributed force the flexibility to operate not just within a limited geographical area but reach beyond the geographical boundaries of what the organic presence force is capable of doing by itself. This is about shaping force domain knowledge well in advance of and in anticipation of events.

This is not classic deterrence—it is pre-crisis and crisis engagement. This new approach can be expressed in terms of a kill web, that is a United States and allied force so scalable and responsive that if an ally executes a presence mission and is threatened by a ramp up of force from a Russia or China, that that presence force can reach back to relevant allies as well as their own force structure in a timely and effective manner.

The P-8/Triton dyad lays a solid foundation for the wide range of innovations we can expect as the integrated distributed force evolves: expanded use of artificial intelligence or AI, acceleration of the speed for software upgradeability, achieving transient combat advantage from more rapid rewriting of software code, an enhanced ability to leverage the weapons enterprise operating from a wide variety of air, ground and naval platforms (off-boarding), and an ability to expand the capabilities of manned–unmanned teaming and collaboration as autonomous maritime systems become key elements of the maritime force in the years to come.

In short, the Maritime Patrol and Reconnaissance Force is not simply transitioning but transforming. It is delivering significant new capabilities now and laying a solid foundation for the future. It is empowering what the Aussies would call a fifth-generation multidomain combat force.

Visiting Jax Navy, 2016

With Ed Timperlake, June 3, 2016

The United States and its core allies are transforming systems, which tend to operate separately but then networked to gain greater synergy to ones which are from the ground up designed to operate as a seamless offensive-defensive enterprise. It is clear when you visit P-8/Triton Patrol and Reconnaissance Wing ELEVEN that the Navy is building their new MDA capabilities from the ground up as a seamless module in a broader strike and defense enterprise.

When we visited Jax Navy, we started our two-day visit with a discussion with Captain Anthony Corapi, the Wing Commander. He has six squadrons all of which have transitioned to P-8 and are in the process of integrating a Triton Squadron into the Wing. He is merging P-8 with Triton into a new approach to provide strike-enabled MDA or MDA-enabled strike, whichever way the flow needs to go.

In our discussion with Captain Corapi, we discovered how the evolution of the P-8/Triton dyad was subsuming within it several of the earlier capabilities flown by the USN to do ASW but was doing so from the standpoint of creating a whole new digital capability, one which could be seamlessly integrated with the air and maritime forces. It is not just a Navy asset; it is a joint and combined warfighting capability, both informed by and informing the entire force operating in the extended battlespace.

It is also clear that the USN by deploying the P-8/Triton prior to the F-35 is coming at the redesign of airpower for the fleet from the perspective generated by the P-8/Triton "internationally" oriented approach as well. The P-3 community is one of the most internationally oriented of any in the USN; it is clear that this tradition is crucial to the P-8/Triton rollout and operation as well.

We started by simply discussing the point that the P-8 really is not a P-3 replacement. "As I transitioned and learned how to fly the P8, I was still using like a P3. It's hard to break 3000-plus hours of flying in a P3 and looking at it as something radically different. I've had to even teach myself that this is not a P3 replacement.

"What struck me the most when I got on board the aircraft for the first couple of flights is how it is so integrated into a network. For years, the P3 was alone and unafraid. It was really good at doing it. It had some good sensors at the time, but it's ability to be networked was very, very minimal."

And change is coming rapidly as many of the crews of the P-8 have never operated on a P-3.

"This airplane is completely different. It is much more automated, so much more. Everything is just set up so much different in the cockpit, just in particular. We're finding that the aircrews are making that leap with really no issue. Because there's so many young aviators now that have never seen a P3 and they're innovating from the ground up, they're learning how to fight the airplane in a completely different way. These young crews do not know what they don't know. They are not unlearning P-3 behavior; they are shaping new behavior appropriate to the digital age."

The combat learning cycle undergone by the P-8 Wing and by the coming Triton squadrons is convergent with the software upgradeable nature of the new air systems. All of the squadrons in the Wing are the baseline P-8. Soon these baseline aircraft will be upgraded to Increment 3. Increment 3 will enhance the networking and communications capability of the aircraft.

But the core point is that even the baseline aircraft is better than and different from the P-3 from the ground up and the crews are learning the skill sets for a P-8, rather than staying within the boundaries of what a P-3 can do and how it operates. "From the beginning, the newbies are learning P-8. Now you have a generation of aviators that have never been inside of a P-3. Actually, I try to make them go onboard every once I a while to give them some appreciation and say, 'This is where you came from. This is your heritage.' But they're learning to take this airplane in directions that wasn't even really intended to go."

We then discussed the acquisition strategy of the P8. "In 2005, we snapped a chalk line and we said, 'Technology, as it exists today, is what goes in this airplane.' We'll do the spiral upgrades later. It was a brilliant move."

He provided an example of how they operate differently. When an operator on the P-8 sees anomalies but is not certain of what they are, the photo can be sent back at the speed of light for input. "For example, on an ASW mission an acoustic operator looking at his displays as he's tracking a submarine, and he sees a line and he's not really sure what it is. He wasn't briefed on that frequency. He takes a snap picture of it on his screen, He sends it back to the tactical operations center. He says, "Hey, I need you to take a look at this line. I wasn't briefed on it. I'm not sure if it's contact or was it something else? What is it?" Then they're able to go do some more in-depth research because they're on the beach, he's flying. They figure out its noncontact. And they go back to the operator and say, "It's noncontact. Disregard."

We asked him to provide more detail with regard to the Increment 3 Upgrades. "We will have access to wideband sat communications which will give us a bigger data pipe and over the horizon reach. We will have the ability to push our communications over the horizon."

Even though the networking is getting better, they are training to operate in the electronic magnetic warfare maneuver space. The crews are being trained to execute commanders or mission intent and not have to rely on networks to execute their missions. In other words, they are training from the ground up to operate in denied communications space.

"The downside of being so networked is you get very used to it. You get very comfortable with the fact that I can talk to anybody, on any network, whenever I want. You may not be able to.

"Not only because it's denied but also for protection. In electronic maneuver warfare, you want to keep the enemy guessing as to exactly where you are. We're starting to go back to the future and teach these kids what it's like to take commander's intent and go out and execute with very little guidance. I'm getting my crews used to the fact where I'll give them commander's intent, I'll give them a pretty good brief, and then I'll turn everything off. I'll say, "Go. Go and operate. You have commander's intent. I want to see them think."

Notably, the ability to network with space assets is a force multiplier, but what can be missed is that the P-8/Triton, F-35, Advanced Hawkeye airborne network can provide a powerful alternative in the case of disruption of space networks.

The P-8s as a multinational aircraft also brings significant expanded MDA capabilities to the allied or coalition force. "If we are truly in a networked environment with the same type model series, built on the same backbone, with these airplanes are all talking to each other, we can have incredible SA. It's better than it was back in the height of the Cold War where it was sector ASW. Then a submarine would come out over the North Atlantic, from the Kola Peninsula, and it was handed off from one sector to another to monitor. Now we can integrate the common operational picture over extended range. It is the reach of the COP; not simply the range of the individual P-3, flying alone and unafraid. We can have a layered picture across from the North to the Central Atlantic."

The Wing is working with the surface fleet to expand the fleet's knowledge of what P-8/Triton can bring to the surface fleet. Indeed, a key question is emerging as fifth-generation capabilities come to the fleet along with the other key software enabled and networked assets: how does the air power transformation reshape what the surface fleet can do and can contribute to operations in the expanded battlespace? And this is not just about ORGANIC carrier airpower; it is about airpower both joint and coalition as well.

A key development will be to reshape the shooter–sensor relationship. Rather than focusing on what weapons are carried on the P-8, the focus can be upon sensing the target and distributing the strike function. "We will see this earliest in the ASW community as we task ASW helicopters to lay ordinance on targets. It will take time to get used to doing that with fast jets or surface assets. But we will get there."

With the P-8/Triton becoming a high value asset, fighter protection will be an important part of the operational experience of the evolving offensive-defensive enterprise as well. "The P-8 is becoming an organic asset of the strike group. It is part of its combat reach and integrated into their networks as well."

Because Captain Corapi is in the process of integrating the first Triton Squadron into a P-8 Air Wing, we discussed how he saw the process of integrating P-8 with Triton as well. He highlighted two key points. First, the

Triton will be operated by crews with P-8 experience and would represent their shore duty. Even though they will be in Jax, they will operate the aircraft in the battlespace. He saw this as important to shaping the career paths of young crewmen and officers who would not like to be stovepiped into an "unmanned career." "It's the Starbucks generation, right? They all like choices. Truly, you have to embrace that mentality. If you look them into one career path, they'll fight it. They don't want that. They want to know they have choice. So far, that's the feedback we've been given is, hey, just let us choose."

Second, with the two systems, the various aspects of electronic warfare deployed earlier via various aircraft can be subsumed and evolved from the two platforms, notably working with the Advanced Hawkeyes and the F-35s. The first two operational birds will be baseline aircraft, largely radar birds. They will go operational rather than going through Initial Operational Test and Evaluation (IOT&E). After the baseline, the following birds will have Electronic Intelligence (ELINT) capabilities built in.

And he reminded us that the Triton was a Remotely Piloted Vehicle, not an unmanned one. When VUP 19 is full up and running, the program of record for VUP 19 is three orbits, and an orbit is 24/7 365 in an orbit; when it's up and running it will have fifth fleet, sixth fleet, and then the homeland defense East Coast orbit, "That's three orbits. The command will approach over 500 people. That's a pretty big manned command. It just means that there's no one flying it in the actual cockpit. It's just flown from a box, but it is very much a manned platform."

The "Family of Systems"
With Ed Timperlake, May 26, 2016

On May 23 and 24, 2016, we visited Jacksonville Naval Air Station and spent time with the P-8 and Triton community which is shaping a common culture guiding the transformation of the ASW and ISR side of Naval Air. The acquisition term for the effort is a "family of systems" whereby the P-3 is being "replaced" by the P-8 and the Triton Remotely Piloted Aircraft.

But clearly the combined capability is a replacement of the P-3 in only one sense—executing the ASW function. But the additional ISR and C2 enterprise being put in place to operate the combined P-8 and Triton capability is a much broader capability than the classic P-3.

Much like the Osprey transformed the USMC prior to flying the F-35, the P-8/Triton team is doing the same for the USN prior to incorporating the F-35 within the carrier air wing.

The P-8/Triton capability is part of what we have described as twenty-first-century air combat systems: software upgradeable, fleet deployed, currently with a multinational coalition emerging peer partnerships. Already the Indians, the Aussies, and the British are or will be flying the P-8s and all are in discussions to build commonality from the stand-up of the P-8 forward.

Software upgradeability provides for a lifetime of combat learning to be reflected in the rewriting of the software code and continually modernizing existing combat systems, while adding new capabilities over the operational life of the aircraft. Over time, fleet knowledge will allow the USN and its partners to understand how best to maintain and support the aircraft while operating the missions effectively in support of global operations.

Reflecting on the visit there are several takeaways from our discussions with Navy Jax. A key point is how the USN is approaching the P-8/Triton combat partnership, which is the integration of manned, and unmanned systems, or what are now commonly called "remotes." The Navy looked at the USAF experience and intentionally decided to not build a the Triton "remote" operational combat team that is stovepiped away from their P-8 Squadrons. The team at Navy Jax is building a common MDA and Maritime Combat Culture and treats the platforms as partner applications of the evolving combat theory. The partnership is both technology synergistic and aircrew moving between the Triton and P-8.

The P-8 pilot and mission crews, after deploying with the fleet globally can volunteer to do shore duty flying Tritons. The number of personnel to fly initially the Tritons is more than 500 navy personnel, so this is hardly an unmanned aircraft. Hence, inside a technological family of systems there is also an interchangeable family of combat crews.

With the P-8 crews operating at different altitudes from the Triton, around 50K, and having operational experience with each platform, they will be able to gain mastery of both a wide scale ocean ISR and focused ASW in direct partnership with the surface navy from Carrier Strike Groups, Amphibious Ready Group (ARG)/Marine expeditionary units (MEUs) to independent operations for both undersea and sea surface rather than simply mastering a single platform. This is a visionary foundation for the evolution of the software upgradeable platforms they are flying as well as responding to technological advances to work the proper balance by manned crews and remotes.

The second key point is that the Commanders of both P-8 aviators and the soon-to-be-operational Triton community understand that for transformation to occur the surface fleet has to understand what they can do. This dynamic "cross-deck" actually air to ship exchange can totally reshape surface fleet operations. To accelerate this process, officers from the P-8 community are right now being assigned to surface ships to rework their joint concepts of operations. Exercises are now in demonstration and operational con-ops to explain and real world demonstrate what the capabilities this new and exciting aspect of Naval Air can bring to the fleet. One example was a recent exercise with an ARG-MEU where the P-8 recently exercised with the amphibious fleet off of the Virginia Capes.

The third key point is that the software upgradeability aspect of the airplane has driven a very strong partnership with industry to be able to have an open-ended approach to modernization. On the aircraft maintenance and supply elements of having successful mission ready aircraft, it is an important and focused work in progress both inside the Navy (including Supply Corps) and continuing an important relationship with industry, especially at the Tech Rep Squadron/Wing level.

The fourth point is how important P-8 and Triton software upgradeability is, including concurrent modification to trainer/simulators and rigorous quality assurance for the fidelity of the information, in shaping the future of the enterprise. The P-8s is part of a cluster of airplanes that have emerged defining the way ahead for combat airpower which are software upgradeable: the Australian Wedgetail, the global F-35, and the Advanced Hawkeye, all have the same dynamic modernization potential to which will be involved in all combat challenges of maritime operations.

It is about shaping a combat learning cycle in which software can be upgraded as the user groups shape real time what the core needs are which they believe require priority in dealing with the reactive enemy. All military technology is relative to a reactive enemy. It is about the arsenal of democracy shifting from an industrial production line to a clean room and a computer lab as key shapers of competitive advantage.

The fifth point is about weaponization and its impact. We have focused for years on the need for a weapons revolution since the U.S. forces, and as core allies are building common platforms with the growth potential to operate new weapons as they come online. The P-8 is flying with a weapon load out from the past, but as we move forward, the ability of the P-8 to manage off board weapons or organic weapons will be enabled.

For example, there is no reason a high-speed cruise or hypersonic missile on the hard points of the P-8 could not be loaded and able to strike a significant enemy combat asset at great distance and speed. There might be a day in future combat when P-8s crews will receive a Navy Cross and Presidential Unit Citation for killing not only an enemy sub but also a P-8 crew sinking a significant enemy surface combatant.

In short, the P-8/Triton team are at the cutting edge of naval air transformation within the entire maritime combat enterprise. And the USN is not doing this alone, as core allies are part of the transformation from the ground up.

Visiting Jax Navy, 2020

July 2, 2020

During a June 2020 visit to Jax Navy, there was an opportunity to talk with Capt. Pottenburgh, Commodore of Patrol and Reconnaissance Wing ELEVEN, and Captain T. J. Grady, Commanding Officer of VP-30 and the Triton Fleet Introduction Team. The two leaders have worked together on and off again throughout their careers, and that collaboration informs and helps synchronize their current efforts as well. And both early on were part of the transition from P-3 to the P-8 and involved in the "training wheels" phase of P-8 development from 2012 through approximately 2017 and the next phase of the deployment of a global fleet and fleet wide modernization efforts since that time.

Obviously, introducing a significantly different aircraft from the P-3, one which operates most effectively embedded in networks, is a challenge. It is challenge on several levels.

The first challenge is working through the kinks in the aircraft itself and getting that aircraft fully functional to deliver the baseline capabilities that the aircraft as a fleet might provide. That takes time for the operators, the operational crew, and the maintainers, to gain the experience to inform the engineers and the contractors of what needs to be fixed, improved, or replaced. That initial phase has been completed, but because it is a software upgradeable aircraft, there is an ongoing quality of what will change onboard the aircraft to adjust to the kill web operational realities of the aircraft within the fleet going forward.

The second challenge is training to operate an aircraft operating with a very different concept of operations than the P-3 which operated "alone and unafraid." Given the nature of the operational capabilities of the aircraft, and how the cabin is configured for operators, there has been a learning process to sort through the kind of crewing and squadron size most effective.

This phase is now under the belt for the Maritime Patrol and Reconnaissance community. And operating the aircraft over time has led to different crewing approaches as well. When we visited Jax Navy in 2016, there were five workstations onboard the aircraft. This now has been increased by one, or to having six workstations onboard the aircraft. They have added a second Electronic Warfare Operator or EWO to the operational crew onboard the P-8.

The third challenge is to adapt the enterprise not simply the P-8 as a platform. Clearly, mastering an ability to operate the P-8 as a platform and one embedded in a kill web is the bedrock from which enterprise management can then be addressed. But because this is a sensor generating, receiving and embedded platform which is both a sensor and shooter, but a sensor-shooter that can enable third-party targeting, the enterprise is an important part of the man, train, and equip function as well.

Part of this challenge is to work ways to manage data much more effectively in support of the MPA fleet as well as the larger joint combat force. This has led to the standing up of Tactical Operations Control Squadron (TOCRON) 11 as part of the Patrol and Reconnaissance Wing as well. This command is operational in June 2020 and is the latest member of CPRW-11. The squadron is tasked with data support and management for CPRW-11. They are tasked with imaging all of the fleet's mission systems hard drives, and data with regard to software, mission planning, and the flight profiles of the fleet. They are the key enabler to maritime patrol's Tasking, Collection, Processing, Exploitation, and Dissemination (TCPED) process, which helps drive the intelligence analysis cycle. With the increase in mission system's capability and increasing integration into the joint kill web, the MPRF community clearly relies on TOCRON with a P-8-enabled MPA force.

The fourth challenge is standing up of the Triton squadron and working the challenge of the co-development of Triton with the P-8 to deliver the common operating picture enabling the kill web force. The Triton is the new kid on the block and is working through the "training wheels" phase much like the P-8 faced earlier.

But the Triton poses other challenges associated with the evolving nature of the enterprise.

How to manage orbital concepts of operations along with more traditional sortie generation operations by manned aircraft? While the P-8 can operate with autonomy and networkability, the Triton is network generating and enabling asset. CPRW-11 and VP-30 works cross-training for the operators for the P-8 and Triton, as the Navy does want to create an isolated remote-piloted operating community.

The Triton puts significant demands on the wave forms and networks enabling the Maritime Patrol and Reconnaissance, and the equip function here certainly reaches beyond what the P-8 and Triton platforms organically carry themselves.

What is being shaped are coordinated operations between the two platforms, where the Triton can sweep the field of operations to identify targets and allow the P-8s to focus on those targets and to focus their activity from take-off on where they need to go and what they need to do. By training operators in both Triton and P-8 operations, crews gain first-hand access to the wider range vision which Triton delvers compared to P-8.

In short, the evolution of the Maritime Patrol and Reconnaissance community poses significant challenges in mastering evolving platforms, notably ones designed to work together. But even greater challenges are posed by the question of training for how that community operates within a distributed maritime force to deliver integrated effects.

Shaping a Way Ahead for the MPA Enterprise

June 30, 2020

Ed Timperlake and I visited Jax Navy almost four years to the day of when I visited Jax Navy this month. In 2013, the first P-8 squadron prepared for deployment; and this year (2020), the 100th P-8 was delivered to the Navy. When we visited in 2016, the Navy had only three years of deployment under its belt and the partner of the P-8, the Triton, was not operating as it is today in the Pacific.

During the 2016 visit, we got a clear sense of how the fighting Navy was re-calibrating to deal with the new strategic context, in which it was spearheading the new generation ISR and anti-submarine fight. During that 2016 visit, all the squadrons in Wing 11 were baseline P-8s. Now four years later, the software upgradeable aircraft has evolved, and the capabilities of the now global fleet of P-8s as well. My recent visit provides a series of insights into the evolution over the past few years, as well as the nature of the foundation being laid for the next leap of capabilities within the fleet and the joint force.

For the P-8/Triton combination is clearly a key capability for the dynamic targeting, which the USAF and the USN are focusing upon for deterrence in the new strategic environment. In a number of the interviews conducted at Jax Navy and Mayport, I had a chance to discuss with P-8, Triton, Seahawk crews, and with a MISR officer how the Navy is leveraging these capabilities to shape a kill web approach for the fleet.

Discussions with CDR Mike Kamas, Commanding Officer, Maritime Patrol, and Reconnaissance Weapons School and his Executive Officer, CDR Matt Griffin, who assumed command of MPRWS on July 24, 2020 highlighted the way ahead for the force. Both Naval aviators have a wide range of operational experience and are clearly leveraging that experience in shaping a way ahead for the maritime patrol enterprise as a plank holder in a kill web enabled maritime force.

CDR Mike Kamas has twenty years of USN service in a variety of roles. Starting out his career as a P-3 Naval Flight Officer at VP-16 in Jacksonville, he has also operated aboard aircraft carriers, served as a flag aide at the Undersea Warfighting Development Center in San Diego, and worked with the surface warfare community in Hawaii. He has operated forward in Europe and the Middle East, providing ISR to the joint force during the land wars of the past two decades. He also served as a Staff Officer at the United States Africa Command as well. In 2017, CDR Kamas came back to Jacksonville, made the P-3 to P-8 transition, and assumed command of the Maritime Patrol and Reconnaissance Weapons School.

CDR Kamas noted that even though the mission sets for the P-3 and P-8 were similar, ASW, surface warfare support, and maritime ISR support, the approach is radically different. The P-8 is part of a wider sensor network, which is interconnected through various C2 links and the platform shapes innovative new ways to do third-party targeting, or essentially operated as part of interactive kill webs rather than like the P-3, which flew "alone and unafraid."

His XO is CDR Matt Griffin who came from an ROTC background at Ohio State. He first deployed from Brunswick Maine as a Naval Flight Officer with VP-26, a P-3C squadron primarily supporting ASW. Midway through this tour, the focus of the squadron's effort transitioned to support the land wars of Operations Iraqi and Enduring Freedom in support of the joint force. During his time in the Gulf, he became familiar with the challenge of operating in an area which is full of ships of varying sizes, purposes, and capabilities, which, of course, is a major challenge facing the U.S. and allied maritime forces in the Pacific.

CDR Griffin noted that even while involved in the Middle East, the Navy made sure that his team's ASW skill sets did not atrophy too much. For example, during one of his deployments, his team was sent to Japan for a period of time to work ASW even while their primary mission had shifted to overland ISR for the joint force. He later went to the Undersea Warfighting Development Center in San Diego where new staff members received insight from very experienced commanders who did ASW in the Cold War period as well. "We were learning from retired Naval officers with hours and hours and hours of real-world operations against adversary submarines."

After his time at the Undersea Warfighting Development Center, he went to serve on the staff of a Destroyer Squadron (DESRON). There he worked on the challenge of translating the language and world of the MPA community into the language and world of the black shoe navy community. Obviously, this translation challenge becomes an important part of ensuring an ability to work effectively third-party targeting capabilities. And these capabilities are emerging from being able to leverage the networks and wave forms empowering effective distributed strike and sensing collaboration.

CDR Griffin then went to NAWDC where he served for two years as the P-3 WTI program coordinator. This added the integration with the carrier air wing aspect to his training and education, in which the fast jet pilots also need to relearn their roles within a kill web concepts of operations whereby interactive networks both inform their targeting and guide their roles in the kill web going forward. And with the sensor rich F-35 coming to the fleet, the role interactions among F-35, Triton, and P-8 is reshaping significantly how the fleet can operate as a distributed integratable force. Next, he transitioned to the P-8 and on his first deployment was intercepted by the Chinese Air Force in the South China Sea.

Both Commanders underscored that for the MPA community their home cycle readiness focus is geared toward dealing with peer competitors. "We practice killing submarines and surface ships with a larger fight in mind." They both emphasized as well that the sensor networks are evolving and within that context the MPA community is learning new ways to shape interactive approaches within the fleet and in the joint community to manage ISR and strike capabilities.

A key aspect which often gets lost when addressing the competition with China is the importance of the combat experience of the joint force being taken forward to provide a combat advantage. I asked them how they looked at how their combat experience from the land wars is leverageable going forward to the new strategic environment. The answer: experience in adaptability and agility.

CDR Kamas noted that during his time in the Middle East, they would operate a significant amount of new roll on and roll off gear on their P-3s. "The gear would be new to us, and we never trained for it during our home cycle. We learned on the fly. The level 500 instructors would shape a rapid learning course and we were able to fly a new technology in a very short period of time. We flew missions in strange places the P-3 was never designed to operate in, and that kind of learning and the incorporation of new technology rapidly is a skill set we are taking forward toward current and future variants of the P-8 Poseidon and MQ-4 Triton."

The P-3 ended up being a global aircraft. The P-8 fleet is being built out as a global fleet, and there is a concerted effort to provide for greater information sharing and interoperability with P-8 partners, like the UK, Australia, New Zealand, and Norway. There is a clear effort to do better in this domain than was done with regard to P-3.

And that interoperability can yield a major advantage with regard to expanding the reach of interactive kill webs as well. The two leaders underscored that the P-8 is a key piece in the evolution of coordinated dynamic targeting. "We are agnostic to who the shooter is. We think the P-8 has significant value in a kill web approach."

They emphasized the importance of ongoing modernization as well of the sensor networks within which the P-8 is embedded, including key capabilities such as the sonobuoy sensors.

In contrast to 2016, now the Triton is part of the operating force, and the approach for P-8 is being modified to leverage this capability as well. Here, the opportunity being generated is for the Triton to provide for wide sweep ISR data, with the P-8 then being able to prioritize targets during its time on station. And to get full value out of the P-8/Triton interactivity, the ability to correlate spiral software development on the two platforms is a key opportunity to evolve the overall ISR/strike enterprise.

At the time of the interview, the Maritime Patrol and Reconnaissance Weapons School was executing its seven-week Maritime Weapons and Tactics Instructor (WTI) course, focused not only on current capabilities but also on what the future has in store for the Maritime Patrol and Reconnaissance Force. "A lot of our focus during the WTI course is on challenges like third party targeting and execution of integrated strike tactics. We deep dive the current way P-8s contribute to the kill web and give the class some ideas of how the platform's software and sensor packages will evolve in the next three to five years. This gives the students the opportunity to use their imagination on the role of the P-8A and MQ-4C Triton in a future fight.'"

Third-party targeting for the Navy means that the tac air community now is beginning to appreciate fully what a P-8/Triton dyad can bring to the fight. "They are clearly starting to see all of the goodness that the P-8 and Triton can provide. As a result, our staffs are talking at a significantly greater level than when you were here four years ago." The coming of MISR is clearly a major change as well in bridging the large wing aircraft and tac air communities as well.

But the software upgradeability piece that we discussed four years ago is clearly becoming a more significant part of the way ahead for the MPA community. When we visited Jax Navy four years ago, all of the P-8s were baseline aircraft. Now the community is seeing more rapid advances with software upgrades to changing baseline aircraft.

CDR Kamas noted that they are now able to feed operator input "back to the engineers and resource sponsors to inform the requirements process and software upgrades, in a way that integrates into the spiral software that comes out every two years and the D.C. budget cycle. We keep a running list of software discrepancies that have been observed by the fleet and need to be corrected and we also prioritize new ideas for software features that can fill tactical capability gaps."

CDR Kamas added that they host an annual conference where the fleet operators meet formally to deliberate on the list of desired changes. "We have a contractor that helps us with the rack and stack prioritization process, transfers those suggestions to the program office, and engages with the resource sponsor to fund the top candidates on the list." This approach is laying down the foundations for further fundamental change within the procurement system and the way spiral software upgrades are managed as well. The speed brake is largely the information assurance piece. "The whole process takes time, but it ensures we comply with DoD Information Assurance requirements."

In short, 2013 was the beginning; 2016 laid a solid baseline aircraft to the fleet operational reset; and now we see the foundation being set for a build out of the integrated distributed fleet empowered by interactive kill webs.

How Do I Train to Work in a Kill Web?

June 29, 2020

Kill webs rely on networks, wave forms, connectivity, distributed C2, and platforms which can leverage all of the former. Platforms are the time-space entities which enable the force; integrability allows a distributed force to deliver the desired combat effect.

At Jax Navy, the P-8 operators are trained to be P-8 operators at VP-30 to be proficient at working the platform. VP-30 takes the operators fresh out of flight school and introduces them to the P-8 as a platform and gets them safe to fly and operate in the aircraft. The operators become competent "newbies" on the aircraft, beyond gaining actual operational experience, how then do they train for the higher end warfighting capabilities, which the aircraft can achieve when operating within interactive kill webs?

My guide to thinking through the answer to this question was my guide for my time in Jacksonville and Mayport, Lt. Jonathan Gosselin. He was enlisted navy before being recruited for the Seaman to Admiral Program. He went to The Citadel and then became a commissioned officer. He was an early P-8 officer, entering VP-45 as it became the third squadron to deploy with the P-8 in 2015. He has certainly experienced the "training wheels" phase of deployment and is now a P-8 Weapons and Tactics Instructor at the Maritime Patrol Reconnaissance Weapons School.

When he first deployed, the P-8 was an anomaly. Now it is deployed to all of the COCOMS worldwide. The P-8 global fleet provides ISR, ASW, and Surface Warfare products to the combatant commanders. In his current position, he serves as an innovation, cross-functional team lead where he works with innovation experts, defense industry, and the Navy to shape projects which are then generated for implementation by industry. He works as well on process changes where advances in TTPs can be enabled as well.

For Lt. Gosselin, at the heart of the effort is really understanding, training for and executing third party targeting. He argued that moving from a stove-piped mentality where one is both the sensor and the shooter, to a kill web perspective where the P-8 could provide the sensors for a firing solution, or whether the P-8 would deliver a weapon provided by another asset to perform the firing solution is at the heart of the change.

According to Lt. Gosselin: "What I am working on right now is shaping a curriculum to bring that capability to the MPRA community. We are working to develop con ops and integrate with other platforms such as the B-1, the B-52, and eventually with the B-21. This is where we're trying to go with the force. We've realized that we've put ourselves in a stovepipe, and we have to break ourselves out of that stovepipe and understand that we are not going to win this fight alone. It does not matter who the adversary is. This is a joint fight."

In effect, dynamic targeting across a distributed integrated force is the goal. As Lt. Gosselin put it: "We're talking about taking targeting data from one domain and quickly shifting to another, just like that. I have killed a target under sea. I am now going to go ahead and work the surface target and being able to understand the weapon-sensor pairing network and being able to call in fires from different entities using commander's intent to engage the target. That's what we're trying to do. Get our operators to understand that it is not just a one-piece answer. There may be a time when you have to transfer the action to another shooter."

To do so, he is engaging significantly with the Triton squadron as well to shape a way ahead for kill web dynamic targeting. Lt. Gosselin noted: "With the P-8 and Triton we are able to expand our envelope of SA. We can take that and now take the baseline concepts from what the P-3 did and apply them to a more advanced tactics, techniques, and procedures in the form of integrating with the B-21, the B-1, the F-18's, the F-35 joint strike fighter in a dynamic targeting kill web."

And with regard to the cultural shift, this is what he added: "It's important to talk not about how can I defeat this target, but really it should be, how can we defeat this target? Let's break ourselves out of this stovepipe and understand that I may not always be the best shooter. I may be the best sensor, but I'm not be the best shooter."

The Impact of the Digital Revolution

June 28, 2020

With the coming of the P-8/Triton dyad, as well as with the F-35, the USN is dealing directly with the digital revolution and its impact on modernization through software upgradeability. I had a chance to discuss these developments during my visit to Jax Navy with Lt. Sean Lavelle, who is intimately involved in the software code rewriting challenges for an operational fleet. Lt. Lavelle highlighted how he saw the relationship of transient software advantage to a kill web versus kill chain approach. Software-defined tactics are the key to quickly adding capabilities to different assets that are supposed to work together.

"It's a kill chain vs kill web approach to development. In the kill chain—you devise a new weapon for a shooter, then figure out the sensor you need for the ISR node, then you figure out the network that makes the most sense for data transmission, then you write the messages you'll send from sensor to shooter. After that, you have to try to sequence all the capabilities so that they arrive roughly at the same time.

"Then when you add a sensor or a weapon, you have to teach the sensor asset what the new weapon brings to the table, or vice versa, and how they can maximize it. It's hard for a community to get good at operating their own new sensors or weapons. It's harder to get good at helping another community employ their capabilities. All of that adds so much time to acquiring and fielding new capabilities, so you end up buying weapons and sensors much slower than the pace of what is technologically possible.

"In the kill web—you buy whatever improves your capability as a sensor or a shooter. Period. If there isn't a perfect network to transmit information right away, it's okay. Just write a software-defined tactics application that can leverage information from a basic datalink, has some basic modeling assumptions, and can give the task force a good, ad hoc plan that gets to a local maximum solution.

"The force can figure out the absolute best way to work together as they experiment, we just need an acceptable way to work together that can get the ball rolling."

As Lt. Lavelle underscored: "We actually just did this for a new sensor/weapon combination in less than twenty hours of software development. The application we fielded solved the entire coordination problem for a completely new concept and optimized the sensor/shooter team. It lets the sensor act as a cloud processing node for the team, even if the human in the sensor aircraft isn't really an expert in what the shooter brings to the table. This process means the limiting factor in technology adoption is not the acquisitions process as is typical, but the actual science."

Lt. Lavelle is part of the Weapons School and an officer working the kill web capabilities of the force. The basic software upgradable dynamic operates around block upgrades, which are planned long in advance. He explained: "The ideal acquisitions process is to conduct operations, learn from those operations and then decide what we want to buy based on that experience. The paradigm that the Federal Acquisition Regulation's System (FAR) forces us into doesn't always lend itself to that sort of iterative, learning-oriented acquisitions process."

He then noted that to break that paradigm, they were focusing on a different approach to software upgradeability. As he explained: "Rather than trying to fix the entire contracting process, we are focused on finding ways to engage in-house talent to get more rapid software upgrades driven by operational experience. We want a tighter coupling of operations and software development than is really possible with current acquisitions regulations."

They are focusing on ways to execute in-house software development under PMA-290, the Program Office for the P-8. Within PMA-290 is an office called the Software Support Activity, which Lt. Lavelle and his team works with. There they are focused on building a system on the P-8 where mission system data, including data links, and information generated by the sensor networks goes to the "sandbox" which is a secure computing environment that can take data, process it, and generate decision-making recommendations for the operator or alert them to tactical problems. It does not directly push data to the aircraft, so it is divorced from safety of flight software considerations.

According to Lt. Lavelle: "This allows us to push updates to the sandbox on timescales measured in days or weeks, rather than years. The Weapons School is building the software for the sandbox based on operators' experiences, while the traditional acquisitions enterprise builds the infrastructure to allow that development. The process is that we observe the fleet's problems, we write code to solve those problems, we send the finished application to PMA-290, they do a security analysis, and then they push it back to be integrated onto the aircraft. We are funding this process operationally rather than on a project basis. We have four to six people at the weapons school at any one time who are trained to write software for the sandbox."

How does Lt. Lavelle view the impact and outcome? "The way I think about it is, we're changing the learning cycle for a force. Right now, when we identify a solution to a tactical problem, we allocate training effort to teach the fleet how to implement it. About 5 percent of that effort goes toward teaching operators the theory around the solution and how to implement it. The remaining 95 percent goes toward continuous training to retain currency. If you have to practice a technique in two simulator events per year to retain currency, which is an underestimate for most techniques, you're looking at 8,000 man-hours per year given the roughly 1,000 operators we have in our force and four-hour simulator events.

"That's a huge amount of resources and the end result is that we are just good at the basics and never really advanced anything because it's sort of a treadmill. You need to spend all of your time maintaining basic skills. Adding new skills just requires too many additional resources.

"With the new approach, we find a problem, we still do the initial effort to teach the fleet the theory, but then we write a piece of software that alerts the operator when that problem is presenting itself and gives them *in situ* tactical recommendations. It is much easier to stay proficient at a task if a machine is helping identify problems and recommending a set of reasonable solutions the human can choose from. Instead of 8,000 man-hours per year, each individual might only need to practice a technique every other year, meaning we save 75 percent of the effort we would have spent and can add four times more new skills per year.

"We've already executed this new approach with several tactical problems. In one case, we reduced failures in a particular scenario from 20 percent of instances to less than 1 percent. Rather than a treadmill where we're constantly teaching the basics, we can have a baseline level that's of performance that's very easily maintained. And then we can advance from there much more quickly."

In short, part of the innovation being done in the MPRA community is about reaching toward a much more rapid process of software upgradeability and integrability for the distributed force. And this cycle is being driven by operations, training engagements, and reflections and cycling back to recrafting the aircraft for its next deployment cycle.

The Coming of MISR to the Fleet

August 5, 2020

During my visit to Jax Navy during the week of June 14th, 2020, I had a chance to talk with the first MISR officer deployed to the fleet, LCDR Tracy Maddox. Her call sign is "Mad Dog" and is as she described herself a "VQ" person by trade and an EP-3 operator. She became an MISR officer through her engagement at NAWDC and worked with "Two Times" there as well. She was involved in the standing up of the MISR cell at NAWDC, which has now become a full warfighting course. She now is with VPU-2, a heralded squadron in the USN involved in "special projects."

LCDR Maddox noted that the EP-3 community works closely with the USAF, so this has carried over for the MISR community and in terms of NAWDC working with Nellis as well. But she clearly highlighted the challenges to getting the USAF and the USN to work fully together in shaping enhanced integratability, but clearly the MISR standup was an important step in moving in that direction.

LCDR Maddox was posted to the USS George H. W. Bush CSG-2 under the command of Rear Admiral Kenneth Whitesell, now commander of Naval Air Forces. During that deployment, the Admiral explored ways that a MISR approach could enhance the lethality of the fleet. The experience shaped a demand side as well where as Vice Admiral Miller put it, there is desire to have MISR officers in every carrier strike group and at the fleet level as well.

And technology needs to be shaped to allow for this kind of innovation. A case in point clearly is Minotaur. LCDR Maddox underscored from her point of view that bringing the various wave forms into a single screen via Minotaur allows those data streams to come together and to shape a common operating picture. She underscored that with different assets using different operating pictures the full value of the ISR streams was not being realized. "With the Minotaur web everyone has access to the same COP regardless of whether you are airborne or onboard a ship."

The MISR incorporation in the fleet, plus the coming of Triton are opening the aperture in understanding of how to widen the scope of what a fleet can achieve within the extended battlespace. And this is clearly a cultural shift as well. As LCDR Maddox put it: "It's a very different mindset shift."

With regard to the carrier strike groups, the core focus has been upon the fast jets and kill chains. But with the ISR/C2 revolution and the ability to do third party targeting, the kill web is becoming a reality. But this means that the Admirals who have come through the fast jet community are facing the challenge of changing their approach as well to incorporate MISR and dynamic targeting, ultimately in a joint capability environment.

The standing up of MISR is significant in and of itself but lays a foundation for the way ahead. This is also a significant generational change as the digital natives become more prevalent within the fleet, and who experienced rapid apps upgrades and want to see the same being delivered in terms of knowledge to the fleet operating in a dynamic combat environment.

From Top Gun to TOCRON

July 7, 2020

For some, the shift from using kill web instead of the kill chain is a variant of wordsmithing. But it is not. I have worked on fifth-generation aircraft since the mid-2000s and certainly understood what an impact a data-rich aircraft flying as a fleet would make with the coming of the F-35. I also understood that if the infrastructure was not built to manage data, and to exploit data much more effectively and rapidly, that the impact of the new generation of aircraft would be limited. I also have argued that fifth-genera-tion aircraft was leading to the "renorming of airpower," and not the end point of transformation.

But what this new generation of aircraft posed along with their being built around software upgradeability was a significant challenge to rethink the ISR/C2 dynamic and to build out an infrastructure, which allows for the platforms operating within interactive kill webs to deliver combat effects throughout the extended battlespace. For the P8/Triton community, what this has meant is that after managing the initial P-8 transition and now adding the Triton in its early phases of deployment is that infrastructure is changing as well to find ways to better exploit the new platform capabilities.

The problem is that if one focuses on the pictures of the aircraft—whether P-8 or Triton—one is looking at a snapshot of a part of the kill web enterprise but missing in many ways the most significant aspect which is the evolving infrastructure. The infrastructure is not as dramatic as watching a plane take off or land, but it is the enabler for the kill web enterprise. It could be put as well in terms of the combat eco-system into which the platform is inserted, leverages and contributes.

In the case of the P-8, a squadron deploys with at Mobile Tactical Operations Center. These centers support the P-8s by managing data and air tasking orders. The infrastructure engagement is a key driver of the way ahead for the maritime patrol reconnaissance enterprise in playing its proper role within a kill web force. And since the initial P-8 deployments and the coming of the Triton, the USN has changed two key aspects of the infrastructure.

The first is the establishment of the MISR officer who is the link between the carrier strike group and the nonorganic assets which are both supporting and supported assets for the carrier strike group. And the second is the current standing up of two TOCRONs for the maritime patrol reconnaissance enterprise. Not surprisingly, the TOCRONS are evolving from the Mobile Tactical Operations Center (MTOC) experience, but are being stood up as a recognition that the data management side of the enterprise is at least on equally footing with the flying side of the enterprise.

The MISR officers are the connectivity tissue between the TOCRONS and the carrier strike group as well. This will be a two-way street as tasking coming from MISR officers will be shaped in part with regard to the kind and quality of information which the TOPCRONS can provide as well.

And as the USMC works its deployed C2 capabilities, and ISR processing capabilities, it would a great deal of sense to find ways for the mobile TOCRON capabilities to merge with or become very synergistic with the USMC deployed capabilities as well.

During my visit to Jax Navy the week of June 14th, 2020, I had a chance to discuss with the TOCRON-11 leadership the role of the squadron. I met with CDR Donte' Jackson and LCDR Heriberto Cruz, both experienced officers in the MPA community and with regard to the working relationship between P-8 and Mobile Tactical Operations Centers or MTOC squadrons.

A key point made by the officers was the importance of socializing the value of the kind of data which the MTOC, MISR, and MPA communities could bring to the fleet. As CDR Jackson underscored: "Sometimes we get caught up in the new systems and what they can do and neglect the core function of leading the sailors who will use the capabilities which the new systems can deliver to the fleet." He sees this as one function of what the TOCRON squadrons could bring to the Navy.

Mission support in terms of what the data providers bring to the fight is crucial to shaping an effective way ahead, and certainly in terms of what a kill web approach can do to empower the fleet. But being data providers does not have the cache of being a Top Gun pilot, but as the data providers become more crucial, a process of change is underway.

The officers underscored that there is significant generational change underway that intersects with the evolving role of the MPA community. On the one hand, "Sailors are well versed in ASW, ISR and C2," not just classic ASW functions in the MPA community. On the other hand, "the new generation of sailors is able to multitask much more effectively than the older generations. And the new generation functions better when they gain a grasp of the whole within which their basic task is performed."

Thus, the officers argued that there was basic synergy between the evolving technology and the capabilities of the new generation of sailors. And they see the TOCRON squadron as contributing to enhancing this process of synergy, as well. The new face of the kill web Navy is MISR officers, TOCRON squadron members, and the warfighters at the information school at NAWDC.

And the focal point of this outcome is to deliver the right information, to the right person in the right time. Learning how to fight at the speed of light is an ongoing challenge. Adding new MISR and TOCRON capabilities to the fleet are the next steps in shaping a more effective capability to meet this challenge.

VUP-19 and the Coming of Triton to the Fleet

July 5, 2020

The Triton is bringing a whole new layer to the kill web for fleet operations. Operating at high altitude, the Triton is delivering area-wide ISR data for dynamic targeting. Indeed, one way to look at the way ahead for the integrated distributed force is to understand that new platforms are providing interactive ISR and C2 layers for a kill web approach for dynamic targeting.

Ed Timperlake and I argued in a *Space News* story published in 2012, that the global fleet of F-35s would provide a significant ISR/C2 layer for the joint and coalition force, which provided redundancy for the space force as well. The ability of the deployed F-35s—again owned by allies as well as U.S. forces—presents a diversified and honeycombed presence and scalable force. This baseline force is significantly enhanced by reach back to space assets, but the space assets now receive redundancy by being complemented as well by a deployed fleet of flying combat systems.[10]

The Triton provides another layer for a kill web-enabled force able to operate with redundancy and resiliency. But to do so, much like learning how to use a data rich aircraft like the F-35, requires technological changes, data management changes, and cultural changes to leverage what the technology provides. Just having the technology is clearly not enough; training and cultural change are crucial to weave what the new technology COULD do into what the force CAN do.

During my visit to Jax Navy the week of June 14, 2020, I got a number of updates on the progress and challenges facing integrating Triton into the fleet. One of those updates was provided by VUP-19. I met with Lt. Samantha (Thompson) Johnson who transitioned from serving as a P-3 pilot to becoming a Triton air vehicle operator and a weapons and tactics instructor at the Maritime Patrol and Reconnaissance Weapons School in Jacksonville. I also met with LCDR Grant Coddington, the Intelligence Officer for the Squadron.

The first takeaway from that conversation, one which was reinforced by other discussions during the visit, was that the Triton operation much like the first few years of P-8 operation, is in its "wheels phase." There is much to learn about the aircraft, its operations, and the data management challenges being posed by the aircraft as well.

The second takeaway is that the learning process has clarified key aspects of the operational cycle for a Triton orbit. Typically, the squadron operates with five members on a shift: two AVOS or air vehicle operators, two MPOs or Mission Payload Operators and one TACCO or Tactical Coordinator.

---

10   Robbin Laird and Ed Timperlake, "Shaping Redundant Response to U.S. Military Space Capabilities," *Space News* (June 27, 2012).

The third takeaway was that the personnel coming into Triton and "learning to Triton" come from the manned collection platform side of the house, P-3, P-8 or EP-3.

The fourth takeaway is that unlike Global Hawk, which has its own dedicated pipe to deliver data, the Triton is working through the Navy's mission data collection systems. This creates challenges in terms of how to best handle the data and how best to ensure it gets delivered to the right place at the right time.

The fifth takeaway is that as software upgradeable aircraft, one paired with the P-8, the Triton is a work in progress. And with a clear focus on informing dynamic targeting, the Triton community is clearly looking forward to coming of the next major upgrade to the mission payload on the aircraft, namely, a multi-INT capability.

The sixth takeaway is that there is clearly a cultural learning process as well. The MPA community has operated throughout its history based on a concept of operations driven by air sortie operations. The Triton is based on a multi-airplane orbit concept of operations which yields a very different data stream than one gets from an air sortied aircraft. And it is one which is layered between what the space systems deliver and what the sortied air collection platforms can deliver.

The seventh takeaway is that the flying side of the house is a work in progress. Notably, with the weather challenges in the Pacific, learning how to manage weather avoidance for a remotely piloted aircraft is a work in progress.

The eighth takeaway is that the Triton in common with other software upgradeable platforms faces the challenge of concurrency between simulators and operational platforms. The operational platform gets and upgrade earlier than the simulators, but the time lag is greater than it should be to close the concurrency gap as efficaciously as possible.

The ninth takeaway is that the Triton community is starting to build some experiential depth, the kind of depth crucial for the knowledge revolution which the Triton can bring to the fleet. And given that the Triton is engaged in tasking, collecting, processing, exploitation, and dissemination of information in real time, learning how to do this for the fleet is a crucial challenge facing the future of a kill web-enabled force.

And looking forward, as the Triton gains multi-INT capabilities, it will become a more effective platform to contribute to the collaborative effort where multiple sensors can be cross-referenced to provide greater fidelity on targeting, and notably when it comes to smaller vessels of interest as well.

Shaping a Way Ahead for the Triton

July 22, 2020

During my recent visit to Jax Navy, I had a chance to talk with several members of the maritime reconnaissance patrol community about Triton. A particularly insightful discussion was with Joseph Opp, currently the Northrop Grumman Director/Site Lead for Triton at Jacksonville Navy Air Station, who has served in this capacity for the past three years. Previously, Opp served for thirty years in the USN and has been involved while in the service for many years with the maritime reconnaissance patrol community. In this capacity, he has been in Jacksonville for some time, first with VP-30 and now with Northrop Grumman.

Clearly, the USN has worked the relationships between Triton and P-8 to provide a comprehensive ISR/Strike solution set. Triton can provide the long-haul wide-angle view of the battlespace with P-8 and its organic and third-party targeting capabilities playing the focused targeting role. To work coordinated operations, the Triton and P-8 crews need to understand from the ground up how each platform works independently and together, to shape an integratable sensor-striker system.

The Triton can have the dwell time to identify a much wider range of targets than P-8, which then enables P-8 to focus their operation on high-priority targets. In the kind of extended battlespace which has and will emerge, knowing where critical choke points are with regard to an adversary's system or force becomes a priority task. An integratable Triton and P-8 working together can provide significantly greater capability to deliver this outcome, rather than simply operating separately. By having crews which have operated on the P-8 as well as the Triton, they share an ability to do the kind of ISR appropriate for dynamic targeting. By working on one platform, then on the other, it is not so much cross-learning as shaping an integrated knowledge base and skill sets to operate in the ASW kill web. Triton can inform the P-8 before it takes off about the threats in the extended battlespace which the P-8 can then prioritize.

Opp noted the progress that is being made with regard to software onboard the Triton. He noted that the program is continuing to work on new workload software for the Triton operators.

With the amount of surface targets on the ocean today in certain regions of the world, this new software can work with Automatic Identification Systems (AIS) data and other systems to help the operators identify threats to be further studied, evaluated, and potentially targeted. This is akin to the mission systems library onboard the F-35s, but this mission library is prioritizing maritime threats. And of course, such threats are crucial for both the USN and the U.S. Air Force to deal with, as significant threats to the USAF in the Pacific come from the sea.

The Triton as an orbital concept of operations airplane is challenging the data management systems which the USN currently operates. There clearly needs to be progress on the data infrastructure side to better handle real time data and to deliver it to the combat edge to support operations which increasingly face the challenge of fighting at the speed of light.

There is some confusion with regard to EP-3 and Triton. There are those who see Triton as replacing EP-3. Some of the core capabilities of the EP-3 are clearly being brought to the Triton platform, but that platform has a wider range of vision and activities than the EP-3.

The Triton/P-8 dyad poses a significant challenge to reworking the C2/ISR-enabled force. On the one hand, decisions can be pushed to the tactical edge. On the other hand, at the fleet command level decisions need to be made rapidly at the strategic level, whereby determinations of what combination of force is appropriate to the crisis at hand, and how best to aggregate that force effectively. Triton certainly can be a contributor to fleet wide decision-making and at the same time channeling P-8s and other ASW assets (such as the Romeo helicopter) to focus their capabilities on the core targets in the extended battlespace.

But there is another challenge facing both industry and the Navy: how to maximize the advantages generated by an orbit concept of operations set of platforms versus a sortie generated set of platforms? Triton does the first; P-8 does the second; and the USN's legacy is only the second.

It is early days for sorting out how to get the number of aircraft up to do the kind of orbital concepts of operations for which Triton was designed. But without enhancing the data management network side of the challenge, the ability to leverage the data generated by Triton will not be maximized.

Triton like F-35 is not being used in terms of storage of data coming off of the aircraft, which makes little sense if the ISR/C2 side of the force will indeed drive the way ahead for the combat force. The data backbone which was assumed to arrive with Triton is not yet there.

If we move toward LEO constellations to work with Triton to add yet another kill web layer, and if the backbone infrastructure is not in place, we will have technology deployed without a solution to how to capitalize on that technology for the evolving combat force.

There are significant opportunities to make use of the post-mission data which F-35s and Tritons can deliver. But an opportunity without a solution is not a capability for the operational force. The opportunity is clearly there and provided by the new data-rich combat assets.

The Seahawk in the Extended Battlespace

July 12, 2020

During my visit to the maritime patrol reconnaissance community during the week of June 14, 2020, I had a chance to meet with the leadership of the HSM Weapons School, Atlantic based at Mayport. In my discussion with CDR Nathaniel "Velcro" Velcio, the Commanding Officer of the School, we focused on the evolution of the community as the Navy has shifted from its support role in the land wars to operations in the extended battlespace against peer competitors.

The broad point driven home by the CO was that in the land wars, the carrier strike groups were focused on support for the land forces and as such operated close to land. This meant that the Romeo version of the Seahawks were clearly prioritizing the protection of the strike group from close in threats, notably, small boats, and subsurface threats of various kinds.

With the shift to a primary concern for the fight at sea, the strike groups have an increased focus on long range surface warfare in addition to ASW. The Romeo is using its long-range detection capability in support of the strike groups and is working as well with interactivity with other assets which can provide the longer-range capabilities for the offensive-defensive force which a strike group represents. This evolution is a work in progress, as the USN and its coalition partners and the joint force refocus on the challenge of dealing with peer competitors.

The first takeaway from the conversation was the important opportunity which better integration of an asset like the Romeo within the kill web approach can provide for the fleet. With the legacy platform build approach, the focus has been upon data links from that platform to the force, without focusing on integrability.

The coming of the Minotaur front end to manage data streams into a single common operating picture is a key step forward to enhanced integrability which will then enhance the role of the Romeo in supporting the fleet as well. Bringing the various wave forms into a single screen via Minotaur allows those data streams to come together and to shape a common operating picture. With the Minotaur web everyone has access to the same COP regardless of whether you are airborne or onboard a ship.

The second takeaway is that integrability requires training to achieve a common operating understanding as well. The P-8 and Romeo communities are now cross learning by putting their operators in each other's simulators, as well as focusing on more common cross-platform training in Florida as well. Such cross training is reduced though by the fact that their simulators cannot work together. Clearly, as the USN pursues a kill web approach, clusters of platforms that are going to work together to shape a shared targeting solution, need to have their simulators integrate as well.

For example, the P-8, and Seahawk, with the coming of MQ-25 should be able to cross train in the synthetic environment. And other new options, such as the Viper operating with Seahawk would be facilitated by integration in the synthetic or simulated environment as well.

The third takeaway is that integration of P-8. Triton, Seahawk, and Vipers could provide a whole new role for the L class ships. Rather than being greyhound buses, the new LHA's could spearhead a whole new sea denial capability. With Romeos onboard then their ability to integrate with Link-16 enabled Vipers could provide for data flowing from the P-8/Triton dyad and sensors on the MQ-25 to shape new capabilities, simply by wave form linkages, cross-training, and new kill web-enabled concepts of operations. To be clear, integrated operations with L-16-enabled Vipers has the potential to enhance close in defense, which is a key task, which frees up other assets to focus on longer-range surface warfare peer threats.

The fourth takeaway would be that platforms such as the Romeo should have a seat at the table determining which passive sensors should go on platforms operating in the extended battlespace.

For example, the Navy is replacing the C-2 with the CMV-22B. But which passive sensors onboard the CMV-22B would be useful to provide data to the Romeo in its extended range EW/SUW role? CDR Velcio put it: "We tend to focus on the sensors to be put under the glass. But what we should also focus on are the sensors that could be added to a platform, that the air crews will not be operating. We can get a significant combat effect by having the right sensors on a platform, but which do not require operational control by that platform's air crew."

A fifth takeaway is that the United States could make much better use of the global partnerships enabled by a program like the Seahawk. With regard to the Australians, their Romeos and the USN are virtually the same and both forces are working common TTPs. This also means for the

Australians as they rethink the role of their amphibious ships, they can work Romeos with Vipers, if they choose to buy them, into a formidable capability flying off of an amphibious ship, now not just a greyhound bus, but a key part of a sea denial mission. With regard to NATO, there is some commonality in operations. According to CDR Velcio, if the ally in question is operating a dipping sonar system, such as the Canadians do with Cyclone and the Brits do with Merlin, that commonality is even more profound.

In short, by shaping a kill web approach, one rethinks how an asset like the Romeo could be used much more effectively in support of the force in the extended battlespace. And one can also focus on how individual platforms might be modernized more effectively but in terms of the pairings with the other platforms with which they operate and to ensure that they can work in a common synthetic environment as well.

Visiting the Seahawk Weapons School

July 8, 2020

During my visit to Jax Navy and Mayport during the week of June 14, 2020, I visited the Helicopter Sea Combat Weapons School Atlantic with my host, Lt. Lt. Jonathan Gosselin, a P-8 Weapons and Tactics Instructor at the Maritime Patrol Reconnaissance Weapons School.

I had a chance while visiting Mayport to talk with Colin Price, who is the Weapons School Standardization Officer responsible for working to shape and support TTP standardization within the fleet. He is also a next-generation officer so to speak in that he is neither a Cold Warrior nor a land warrior. He has come to the fleet, when the focus is clearly upon the new strategic environment and dealing with the new world of surface and ASW, and within the extended battlespace in the sea–air domain. He has been posted to Japan where he worked the Romeo with the new Naval assets which came to Japan, the new-generation Hawkeye and the F-35. With regard to the new-generation Hawkeye, Price underscored how important cross-learning in the flight line is for tapping into the potential for a new platform and sharing knowledge of how your platform might contribute to the success of the new platform, notably with an integratability focus. With regard to the F-35, the Marines had brought the F-35 Bravo to Japan, and the Romeo squadron flew down to their base and engaged in cross-learning. As Price put it: "It is important to open communication with the operators of a new platform, to have the kind of cross-learning, which can shape more effective concepts of operations, and to get the full combat capability from your platform and the new one."

With regard to getting better value out of the Romeo, Price pointed out that the AN/ALQ-210 Electronic Support Measures System on the Romeo can contribute significantly to EW combat as well, and the Romeo community has recently increased its focus on improving their capabilities with regard to this mission set. As the focus shifts to distributed EW in the force, and away from a primary reliance on a specialized EW platform, then learning how to tap into an integrated EW capability distributed within the force is a key task, one to which the Romeo community can contribute to significantly. To do so, will require shaping the kind of architecture which can more effectively network EW capabilities across the fleet. But the Romeo can provide a significant contribution here, notably when ships are operating in congested waters or close in transit points where fast jets are of more limited value in the EW role.

The basic function of the Romeo is to provide the "Paul Revere" role for the fleet. The Romeo's systems are critical ones for closer in support to the fleet, given the ability of its dipping sonar when combined with the processing power onboard the aircraft to provide rapid warning to the fleet of impeding threats.

As the USN works to shape an interactive kill web force, a key challenge will be to more effectively manage what integratable sensor networks can deliver to the fleet and to the force. Lt. Price argued that when working a Romeo with a P-8, for example, it is important to be able to share track data for a dynamic targeting solution, and especially so, if that track data would be used by a third party to deliver the targeting solution.

Lt. Gosselin underscored that the challenge can be seen as one of layering and sequencing. "How do we layer most effectively our sensors to the point where we get the best quality of target tracks?" With regard to sequencing: "How do we sequence most effectively so that we can maintain a consistent track over a long period of time?" This might be seen as a tactical challenge, but it is clearly one which delivers strategic consequences, notably in terms of determining which targets are the ones which the commander wants to prosecute, and which ones he does not.

It is clear that this is a kill web approach being forged at the source. In this case, it is the P-8 and Romeo communities working to sort through how to work more effectively as an integrated capability for the offensive-defensive enterprise which the Navy needs to deliver in the peer fight and operating in the extended battlespace.

The Fire Scout

While visiting Jax Navy in June 2020, I had the opportunity to talk via teleconference with CDR Gregory Knutson, the CO of the Helicopter Sea Combat Weapons School Atlantic or the HSC Weapons School based in Norfolk. My host, Lt. Jonathan Gosselin had arranged the discussion for a very good reason—not only are the Sierra and the Firescout working in innovative new ways to deliver the desired operational outcome, but there is an important potential to be unlocked by broadening the P-8s working relationship beyond Triton in terms of working with remotely piloted aircraft.

CDR Knutson explained that the Sierras and the Fire Scouts were operating off of LCS ships in support of security missions in the Caribbean. And in those missions, the force package was working in support of Joint Interagency Task Force South. This command is a multiservice, multiagency task force based at Naval Air Station Key West and is under the command of a USCG officer.

The command provides a unified command and control for drug interdiction activities. And its C2 is supported by integrated ISR resources as well, and although focused on security missions provides an interesting model of how integration might proceed in other command areas as well.

In support of JIATF South, Romeos and Fire Scouts work together to prosecute the counter-drug mission. Based on a tasking from JIATF South, a potential counter-drug target is identified. The Fire Scout is sent out to verify that it is indeed a target which needs to be prosecuted. If confirmed, then the Sierra is sent out with a USCG sniper in the back of the helicopter to prosecute the drug smugglers.

The two rotorcraft operate from the LCS with a joint support crew of maintainers. The Fire Scout is managed from the LCS itself and the two rotorcrafts work closely together to pursue and prosecute the identified target. The Fire Scout can also be used to remote designate targets for other assets. For example, with regard to Sierras working with Fire Scout, they can remote designate targets for the Sierra's Hellfire missiles or APKWS rockets. This clearly is an important role in the Pacific and has been used in the past as well in the Mediterranean.

What Fire Scout and Sierras have achieved is an operational demonstration of ways remotes and manned assets can work together to prosecute missions. Certainly, a key way ahead for the P-8 would be to encompass Fire Scout operations as well as Triton operations as a way for paving a way ahead for the expansion of maritime remotes which can be anticipated in the decade ahead.

This is especially important given the challenge which small ships pose to combat ships as well as masking adversarial combat intentions and operations. Sorting through the chaff of maritime traffic and understanding how adversaries mask intentions and capabilities by using smaller ships is part of the challenge moving ahead.

By being able to use an evolving capability of remote sensing assets, the C2 capabilities afloat, in the air or ashore can be enhanced to make timely decisions with regard to desired security or combat outcomes. In other words, the teaming would enhance the capability to prevail in full spectrum crisis management.

Rear Admiral Garvin's Perspective

May 13, 2020

Rear Admiral Garvin leads the USN's global maritime patrol and reconnaissance enterprise. This means that he trains, certifies and deploys the USN's Maritime Patrol and Reconnaissance Forces worldwide in support of theater Fleet and Combatant Commanders. This global oversight provides him a unique opportunity to focus on the entire scope of maritime operations, rather than being focused narrowly upon one particular theater.

A 1989 US Naval Academy graduate, he witnessed the past thirty plus years of change in the political/military environment as a P-3 pilot. This meant as well that he was entering the force coincident with the perceived sunsetting of the Soviet Naval threat and transition to a new era of maritime patrol operations. He began his deployed operational experience at Keflavik, Iceland as part of the U.S. and the North Atlantic Treaty Organization (NATO) Anti-Submarine Warfare (ASW) force prosecuting former Soviet, now Russian submarines. Contrast this with his last operational deployment where he focused almost entirely on over land ISR contribution to the United States Central Command (CENTCOM) forces. Notably, despite the decades-long increase in overland ISR and combat focused missions, the Navy did not abandon its key ASW mission set but those skill sets were not as prominent as they once were.

Question: In a way, the approach we took with our allies to defend the GIUK (Greenland, Iceland, and the United Kingdom), which included the sound surveillance system, manned aircraft, and combat ships of various types, is being morphed today into a 360-degree manned–unmanned teaming tracking and kill web. Is that a fair way to put it?

Rear Admiral Garvin: "It is. We are following a similar mission construct working with our allies but the thinking and modality has advanced significantly. We are taking full advantage of the leap forward in many sensors and communications technology to interoperate in ways that were previously impossible. Faced with a resurgent and challenging ASW threat, we have not given up on the old tool sets, but we are adding to them and weaving them into a new approach.

"We are clearly shifting from linear or sequential operational thinking into a broader understanding and implementation of a web of capabilities. In the past, when operating a P-3, you operated alone, you had to be the sensor and the shooter. To be clear, it remains necessary that every P-8 aircraft and crew be ready and able to complete the kill chain organically, but the fact of the matter is that is not the way it always has to be, nor is it the way that we're planning for it to have to be going forward.

"On any given mission, the P-8 could be the sensor and perhaps the allied submarine is the shooter. Or vice versa. Or maybe the destroyer is the one that happens to get the targeting solution and the helicopter is the one that actually drops the weapon. Sensor, shooter, communications node, or perhaps several at once, but each platform is all part of a kill web."

Question: The P-8 and the Triton are clearly a dyad, a point often overlooked. How should we view the dyadic nature of the two platforms?

Rear Admiral Garvin: "There are several ways to look at this. The first is to understand that both platforms are obviously software driven and are modernized through spiral development. We focus on spiral development of the dyad in common, not just in terms of them as separate platforms. It is about interactive spiral development to deliver the desired combat effect.

"Another key element of teaming is that during the course of their career, the operators of P-8 and Triton have the opportunity to rotate between the platforms. This gives them an innate understanding of the mission set and each platform's capabilities. They, better than anyone, will know what the dyad can deliver, up to an including a high level of platform-to-platform interaction. The goal is to be able to steer the sensors or use the sensor data from a Triton inside the P-8 itself.

"The idea of P-8 and Triton operators working closely together has proved to be quite prescient. Our first Triton squadron, VUP-19 is down in Jacksonville, Florida under Commander, Patrol and Reconnaissance

Wing 11. And when we build out the full complement of Tritons, we'll have VUP-11 flying out of Wing 10 in Whidbey Island, Washington. Triton aircrew literally work down the hall and across the street from their P-8 brothers and sisters.

"The Maritime Patrol and Reconnaissance aviator of the future will be well versed in the synergy inherent in both manned and unmanned platforms. The unblinking stare of a Triton enhances the Fleet Commander's Maritime Domain Awareness (MDA) and understanding of an adversary's pattern-of-life by observing their movements in the optical and electromagnetic spectrum.

"Moreover, Triton serves as a force multiplier and enabler for the P-8. Early in Triton program development, we embraced manned and unmanned teaming and saw it as a way to expand our reach and effectiveness in the maritime domain. One key software capability which empowers integration is Minotaur. The Minotaur Track Management and Mission Management system was developed in conjunction with the Johns Hopkins University Applied Physics Laboratory. Minotaur was designed to integrate sensors and data into a comprehensive picture, which allows multiple aircraft and vessels to share networked information. It is basically a data fusion engine and like many software capabilities these days, doesn't physically have to present on a platform to be of use. These capabilities ride on a Minotaur web where, if you are on the right network, you can access data from whatever terminal you happen to be on."

Question: With such an approach to integratability, then this allows the fleet to be able to collaborate with one another without each platform having to be topped up with organic generators of data and to have to maximize the sensor–shooter balance on a particular platform. This then must provide flexibility as well when flying a dyad rather than a single aircraft to work a broad range mission like ASW?

Rear Admiral Garvin: "It does. It also provides for resiliency through multiple sensor points in the kill web empowering multiple kill points on that web.

"This begs the question, how much resiliency do you want to build in? Do you need several platforms that carry the actual data engine, with the rest of the force simply having access to data produced by the data fusion engine? It becomes a question of cost-benefit and how much resilience do you want to build into each individual platform."

Question: In other words, the new approach allows for a differentiated but integrated approach to system development across the force seen as interactive platforms?

Rear Admiral Garvin: "I think of it this way, rather than taking an evolutionary or iterative approach, what this allows for is a step change approach. We're thinking beyond just the iterative."

Rear Admiral Garvin drove home a key point that the MPA dyad operates in a way that is not simply a USN capability for a narrowly confined ASW mission sets. The United States Air Force (USAF) is clearly concerned with the maritime threat to their air bases and needs to ensure that a joint capability is available to degrade that threat as rapidly as possible to ensure that the USAF has as robust an airpower capability as possible. Certainly, the B-21 is being built in a way that would optimize its air–maritime role. And clearly a bomber can get to an area of interest rapidly and to deliver a customized strike package.

Hence, the new MPA approach is a key part of the evolving USAF approach to future capabilities as well. The color of the uniform perhaps belies how joint a kill web approach to platforms really is.

Extending the Reach of the Kill Web

May 13, 2020

In a follow-up interview with Rear Admiral Garvin, we focused on how the MPA community is working with allies. In effect, what we see coming in the Pacific and in the Atlantic are interactive sensor webs that extend the reach of core platforms and their onboard sensors. The fusing of multiple sensors via common interactive self-healing webs enhances the ability of the entire force, including key partners and allies, cooperatively to engage enemy targets in a time of conflict.

Interactive webs can be used for a wide range of purposes throughout the spectrum of conflict and are a key foundation for full spectrum crisis management. To play their critical role when it comes to strike, whether kinetic or non-kinetic, this final layer of the web needs to have the highest standards of protection possible. The interactive webs enhance the reach of any platform within a task force and thus create synergy among non-contiguous assets that are combined against a specific threat. Interactive kill webs also provide redundancy and depth for distributed operations and inherent resiliency and survivability that a convergent combat force simply will not have.

We started with a discussion of the reach of the maritime patrol enterprise by focusing on a way to conceptualize the way ahead for shaping an integrated distributed force. If one conceptualizes the battlespace as layers of visuals placed one on the other, it becomes clear what is different in terms of leveraging the combat force within an interactive web. The first layer would be the operational geography of the battlespace. The second layer would be the threat elements most relevant to the blue force. The third layer in the case of a maritime patrol enterprise would be commercial maritime shipping traffic. Unlike air traffic, maritime traffic is very diverse and very large and provides a key masking function for any adversary. The fourth layer would be the laydown of blue assets, including the geographic distribution of allied forces in the region or area of interest. The fifth layer would then be where the P-8/Triton dyad operates.

With such a schematic, it is quickly evident that if the USN's P-8/Triton dyad is integratable with allied maritime patrol capabilities, the reach of both the U.S. and allied interactive web capabilities is substantially enhanced. It is also obvious that if key allies are not engaged then there are holes in the web structure which will either simply be gaps or need to be filled by other means. In simple terms, it is clear that the United States and its allies must operate within a convergent set of interactive webs to shape a shared and actionable shared operating picture.

The terms most often used for this is shaping a COP or a "common operational picture," but this challenge is really beyond the ken of most real-world combat maritime missions.

As a senior USMC officer put it in the Fall of 2020: "We do not expect a persistent common operational picture in the future. Rather, in a contested operational environment, where we know that our adversaries are getting good and perhaps better than us, some days as systems confrontation, we know that we have to learn to provide moments of clarity on demand as opposed to that persistent COP. Domains like aviation or air supremacy, where in the past we would mark a good day by sortie generation, perhaps in the future we think that might be replaced by the ability to enable long-range precision fires as a measure of air superiority. And that's going to require robust ISR, over the horizon communications, and the ability to enable sensor to shooter operations."

The results will significantly empower a combined strike force and, even more importantly, inform decision makers about how to prioritize targets in a fluid combat situation. There is a particular and often intellectually neglected part of this problem—the existence of offensive nuclear capability. As an example, in the Pacific, there are three nuclear powers. Nuclear deterrence is woven throughout any considerations of conventional operations, so there is a clear need to add a strategic overlay of the battlespace, which considers potential consequences and focuses on making the right target decisions in a fluid battlespace. This "wildcard" should give pause to those who tout AI-enabled kill chains.

Decision makers need to step back and consider that while more rapid destruction of targets is important, it must be guided by both tactical and strategic decisions with due regard not just to combat but political effects as well in full spectrum crisis management. Having men in the loop in airborne systems, like the Maritime Patrol and Reconnaissance Force (MPRF) can certainly contribute to target discrimination efforts.

We also considered the specific challenges of the USN working with allies in the maritime patrol enterprise. For obvious reasons, we first focused on those allies who have already joined the P-8/Triton dyad effort. We then discussed those allies who had not done so but are key partners in working interactive webs with the United States. Prior to highlighting that discussion, let me review who the P-8/Triton partners are to date.

Australia is the only U.S. ally pursuing both the P-8 and the Triton. As a cooperative partner, similar to the F-35, they participated in the development of P-8A and Triton capabilities from the ground up with the USN. The British have made a very welcome reentry into the Maritime Patrol and Reconnaissance arena with the P-8 as well.

During recent visits to Royal Air Force (RAF) Lossiemouth, I saw the program being stood up in Scotland, and they were doing it in such a way that other P-8 partners would be supported as well. The key role of standing up new infrastructure to support this effort is crucial to handle the new data rich airplanes, as well as the work with allies in operating the assets.

Having visited Norway several times over the past few years and having discussed among other things, the coming of the P-8 and the F-35 in Norway, it is clear that what happens on the other side of the North Sea (i.e., the UK) is of keen interest to Norway. And talking with the RAF and Royal Navy, the changes in Norway are also part of broader UK considerations when it comes to the reshaping of NATO defense capabilities in a dynamic region. The changes on the UK side of the North Sea are experiencing the standup of a P-8 base at Lossie, which will integrate with U.S. P-8 operations from Iceland and with those of Norway as well.

In effect, an Maritime Domain Awareness or MDA highway or belt is being constructed from the UK through Norway. A key challenge will be finding the best ways to share data and enable rapid decision-making in a region where the Russians are modernizing forces and expanding their reach into the Arctic.

The Pacific partnership is being expanded as well with the addition of South Korea. In 2018, the South Korean Government announced that would purchase six P-8s. They are thereby joining India, which has its own systems configured on the aircraft. India's first P-8I squadron was stood up at Rajali in November 2015. The Indian Navy operates its entire fleet of eight P-8I maritime patrol aircraft from Rajali, and the Indian Government announced last year that they intended to buy ten additional P-8s.

With regard to the P-8/Triton partners, Rear Admiral Garvin highlighted the opportunities for co-learning, which are generated from common training that occurs at VP-30 and the Maritime Patrol and Reconnaissance Weapons School at NAS Jacksonville, Florida. He highlighted the famous quote, "You cannot surge trust." The working relationships built during high-end tactical training carry over into operations whereby a global community of operators can share operational experience and enrich development of the global enterprise.

According to Garvin: "My first international visit upon taking command was to Australia, leadership there referred to our working relationship as 'mateship.' This term accurately describes the collaborative nature of our partnership and demonstrates its importance to ourselves and the rest of the world. We have built similar relationships on varying scales, all around the world. These relationships serve as force multipliers, which opens the door cooperatively to leverage technology to deliver networked sensors and a shared understanding of the decisions and options we share across the extended battlespace.

"Our allies understand the fundamental nature of their regions better than we do. If you have properly maintained these important working relationships, both interpersonal and technological, then you will have access to the cultural knowledge and human geography that might otherwise would not be available to you. We become stronger interactively with our allies by sharing domain knowledge to operate across a wider geographical area. In effect, we are shaping kill web 'matesmanship.'

"We clearly have closer relationships with some allies than with others, which shapes policy and data sharing. However, the technology is now out there which can allow us, within the right policy framework, to provide data at appropriate security levels much more rapidly than in the past. Our policy frameworks simply need to catch up with our technologies.

"History has shown us that it is infinitely more difficult to sort out our working relationships in times of intense conflict. Those partnerships need to be nurtured and exercised now to help shape our interactive kill webs into a truly effective strike force over the extended battlespace."

For Rear Admiral Garvin, working with partner and allied maritime patrol partners is crucial, even when those close partners are operating different platforms. For example, Japan indigenously developed their own replacement aircraft for its legacy P-3s. He highlighted the healthy sharing arrangements the USN has with the Japanese Maritime Self-Defense Force in the MDA area. Similarly, the USN enjoys a very close relationship with Canada, who operates a significantly modernized P-3, the *CP-140 Aurora*. He noted that the aperture for increased cooperation with India was opening up as well, a process which he clearly welcomed.

As Rear Admiral Garvin put it: "Put simply, the idea of partners and allies sharing in the web you describe must have, at its core, that underlying, underpinning relationship built upon trust. Sometimes buying the same kit does make it easier. But without that relationship it doesn't matter if you bought the exact same kit."

CHAPTER FOUR:

MAWTS-1 SHAPES A TRANSITION

Overview

January 20, 2020

The significant change in USMC aviation since the introduction of the Osprey has set in motion fundamental changes overall in USMC capabilities and concepts of operations. In the past decade, the Osprey has matured as a combat platform and fostered significant change in concepts of operations. No less than the virtual end of the legacy operations of the Amphibious Ready Group-Marine Expeditionary Unit (ARG-MEU) and the shaping of a new approach to amphibious warfare and shaping new concepts of operations for dealing with peer competitors is underway.

With the end of the primary focus upon the land wars, the Osprey and changes to the attack and support helicopter fleets have transformed how the Marines can operate in a combat space. The revolution in tiltrotor technology and the much more effective integration of the Yankee and Zulu class helicopters have allowed the Marines to have a smaller logistical footprint in covering a wider combat space.

Enter the F-35B. With the coming of the F-35B and the impact of the template of change laid down by the Osprey, with its range and speed, together they are driving significant change in distributed operational combat capability. This capability has been not only reinforced but is being taken to the next level. Now with a Communications, Navigation and Identification (CNI) avionics suite or CNI-enabled aircraft with 360-degree SA, a Marine

Corps MAGTF can deploy with an integrated EW-ISR-C2-weapons carrier and can form the backbone for enabling an insertion force.[11]

In other words, the 2010s have seen the maturing of the tiltrotor revolution being combined with the arrival of fifth-generation capabilities. And the Marines are the only combat force in the world with cutting-edge integration of these new capabilities within the overall combat force.

The success of the 2010s has fostered change in how the USMC was able to operate as a crisis management force. Those successes provide the tip of the spear as well for the innovations of the 2020s. Now the challenge is full spectrum crisis management which requires a force capable in operating in contested air and sea space and with an ability to provide more effective engagement as an integrated distributed force.

It is clear that USAF and USN as well as the U.S. Army are shifting from their legacy forces, which operated in the land wars of the 2010s, to working on becoming an integrated distributed force in which multidomain operations and tactical decision-making at the edge is a core focus of effort and attention.

Yet there is some confusion in the analytical literature over where the Marines are headed with regards to their next round of innovation. For many the focus is upon a more traditional approach to crisis management rather than realizing that the strategic shift is to full spectrum crisis management.

Some analysts have argued that the Commandant's New Guidance is really the end of the crisis management Marines in favor of becoming part of the Navy's overall combat force. Others see the changes in the U.S. Army has encompassing changes which the Marines have made to subsume Marine Corps capabilities and to displace them. As the Army shifts to buying, deploying and adapting to a new generation of high-speed helicopters, some see this as the inevitable outcome.

But in fact, the world has changed. Doing crisis management against adversaries which possess significant strike and defense capabilities clearly requires shaping a more lethal and effective distributed force. And in such a

---

11   Robbin Laird, *Three Dimensional Warriors: Second Edition* (Kindle, 2013).

world, sea-basing integrated with an ability to use flexible land basing is a core capability from which the United States and its core allies can gain an operational advantage. It also provides enhanced capability to do offensive-defensive operations with a distributed yet integrated force.

In his guidance, General Burger, the Commandant of the USMC, speaks of the growing importance of Expeditionary Advanced Base Operations or EABO. "We are going to build a force that can do EABO opposed to building an EABO force."[12] When you couple this with the opportunity to combine the use of the fleet (amphibious, surface, subsurface, Unmanned Surface Vessels (USVs), and Unmanned Underwater Vehicles (UUVs) with islands and allied territory (certainly not only already operational bases), the challenge will be to integrate these capabilities, sea-basing, manned and unmanned, with land bases, temporary or more permanent. Part of the challenge will be to be able to establish Forward Arming and Refueling Points or FARPs and to fold those into the integrated distributed force. Also crucial is to shape C2 mesh networks that can combine distributed forces into a coherent combat force and operate at the tactical edge.

USMC Aviation Innovations for the 2020s

The projected additions of USMC aviation assets in the decade ahead clearly can provide key capabilities to enable this transition, much like the changes of the past decade put the Marines into this position in the first place.

Three key additions are crucial to this evolution. The first is the addition of the CH-53K. Without an effective heavy lift asset, an ability to operate form the seabase or to established distributed FARPs in the operational window for an integrated distributed force, the Commandant's strategy will be undercut. The CH-53K will provide a key element of being able to carry equipment and/or personnel to the objective area. And with its ability to carry three times the external load of the CH-53E and to be able to deliver the external load to different operating bases, the aircraft will contribute significantly to distributed operations.

---

12   "Commandant's Planning Guidance," *38th Commandant of the Marine Corps.*

But the digital nature of the aircraft, and the configuration of the cockpit is a key part of its ability to contribute as well. The aircraft is a fly-by-wire system with Digital Interoperability (DI) built in. And with multiple screens in the cockpit able to manage data in a variety of ways, the aircraft can operate as a lead element, a supporting element or a distributed integrated support node to the insertion force.

A key change associated with the new digital aircraft, whether they are P-8s or Cyclone ASW helicopters, is a different kind of workflow. The screens in the aircraft can be configured to the task and data moved throughout the aircraft to facilitate a mission task-oriented work flow.

In the case of the CH-53K, the aircraft could operate as a Local Area Network for an insertion task force, or simply as a node pushing data back into the back where the Marines are operating Marine Air Ground Tablets (MAGTBs).

Marines carrying MAGTBs onboard the CH-53K will be able to engage with the task force to understand their role at the point of insertion. The K as a digital aircraft combined with the digital transformation of the Marines create a very different ground force insertion capability.

The second is the addition of new and more capable unmanned assets to empower the force, and to provide for the proactive ISR which the integrated distributed force needs to enhance their operational effectiveness.

The third is further progress in shaping the digital integration of the force so that distributed operations can be more effective in contested environments. The significant changes in C2 and ISR capabilities, integration, and distribution is many ways the sixth generation rather than being a new aircraft. For the Marines, working DI has been a high priority as they prepared for the shift from the land wars to engaging in contested multidomain operations.

According to the USMC 2019 Aviation Plan:

"Digital interoperability is the seamless integration of digital systems and exchange of data, across all domains and networks throughout the MAGTF, naval, joint, and coalition forces, to include communication in degraded or denied environments, to share rapidly accurate information, provide greater SA, accelerate the kill chain, and enhance survivability in order to outmaneuver and defeat the threat across the Range of Military Operations (ROMO)…

"The Marine Corps executes mission threads primarily as an integrated MAGTF organized to support the Marine rifleman. The integration of the MAGTF and the successful execution of mission threads relies on the effective exchange of critical information; communication therefore, whether in the form of electronic data or voice, is critical to the exchange of mission essential information…

"We continue to pursue integration and data exchange throughout various arenas: SA; aircraft survivability; intelligence, surveillance, and reconnaissance; fire support; and logistics by conducting continuous and iterative analysis of ever evolving information exchange requirements (IERs) and the technological tools needed to satisfy those requirements."[13]

And it is at MAWTS-1 where innovation is driven by the work of the weapons schools and the training exercises. It is to the role of MAWTS-1 that we now turn.

Col. Wellons, CO of MAWTS-1, 2016

With Ed Timperlake, December 17, 2016

During our 2016 visit to USMC Air Station Yuma, we had a chance to meet with the head of MAWTS-1 and discuss the way ahead for the USMC and its integrated aviation capabilities.

Question: When we were last here, MAWTS-1 did not yet have its own F-35s. Now you do. How are working its integration with the MAGTF?

---

13   *2019 Marine Corps Aviation Plan.*

Col. Wellons: "The great thing about MAWTS-1 is we run the Weapons Training Instructor (WTI) course at Yuma twice a year, and as a former CO of MAWTS put it to me, WTI is where the USMC comes together every year to train for war. We are able to do the high-end training in terms of aviation support to the MAGTF.

"The F-35 is integrated into every mission that we do, whether it is close air support, helicopter escort, or, at the high end, air interdiction operations against a high-end threat including integrated air defense as well.

"When we come back from a typical WTI mission exercise, and we debrief it with the helo and fixed wing guys and the C2 guys and the ground combat guys, more often than not it is the F-35 which is identified as the critical enabler to mission success. It is the SA we gain from that platform, certainly when dealing with a higher end threat like dealing with air defense, that provides us with capabilities we have in no other platform. I am pleased with where we are with the airplane right now. We have declared IOC and we are getting to deploy it to Japan."

Question: How does the integration of the F-35 into your operations, change how you think about those operations?

Col. Wellons: "A lot of that can be quickly classified but let me give you an example, which does not fall into that category. Historically, when we could come off of L class ship with Mv-22s, CH-53s, Cobras, and Harriers and we then faced a serious AAA or MANPADS threat we would avoid that objective area. Now we do not need to do so. It changes the entire concept of close air support. In Afghanistan and Iraq, we have not had prohibitive interference in our air operations. With double digit SAMS as part of threat areas we are likely to go, the F-35 allows us to operate in such areas. Without the presence of the F35, it would be a mission that we wouldn't be capable of executing.

"The SA of the airplane is a game changer for us. Rather than getting input from the Senior Watch Officer on the ground with regard to our broader combat SA, we now have that in our F-35s. This allows us to share SA from the pilot flying the airplane and interacting with his sensors. He can share that information, that SA, with everybody from other airborne platforms to the ground force commander in ways that are going to increase our ops tempo and allow us to do things that historically we wouldn't have been able to do.

"The ability of the F35 to be able to recognize and identify the types of prohibitive threats that would prevent us from putting in assault support platforms and ground forces is crucial to the way ahead. The F-35 can not only identify those threats but also kill them. And that is now and not some future iteration."

Question: You are innovating as well with the F-35 as you integrate with your forces. Can you describe an example of such innovation?

Col. Wellons: "Absolutely. One example has been something we did in the last WTI class, namely hot loading of the F-35 as we have done with the F-18 and the Harriers in the past.

We worked with NAVAIR and with China Lake and Pax River and came up with a set of procedures that we can use to do the hot load of an F-35. We did it successfully at this last WTI class, and it shortens significantly the turn time between sorties.

"When you think about us operating in some places around the world we do, the number of additional sorties we can generate as a result of being able to do that, and the reduction in the vulnerability that we have in terms of the turnaround is crucial. Also, whenever you shut an airplane down, whether it's a fifth-gen airplane or a legacy airplane, it has a greater tendency to break. We did GBU-12 last class, we'll be doing GBU-32 and AIM-120 this upcoming class."

Question: Obviously, you are working with the USAF and the U.S. Navy on reshaping air operations affecting the MAGTF, can you give us a sense of that dynamic?

Col. Wellons: "For the USAF, the capabilities of the airplane in terms of the sensors that we have, the weapons that we have, the way that we're employing this airplane, they're remarkably similar. We are in lockstep with Nellis, with the weapons school, with the 53rd Tests and Evaluation Group in terms of how we're doing operational tasks, and we are very closely aligned with them in terms of how we employ the airplane, how we support the airplane.

"We do quite a bit of work with Fallon. They are on a different timeline from the Air Force. They're a couple of years behind in terms of where they are, but I anticipate that we'll have similar collaboration with the Navy as they begin to lean forward into the F35 in the next couple of years."

Col. Wellons, CO of MAWTS-1, 2018

June 1, 2018

The WTI's at MAWTS-1 have become especially significant as the Marines are going through the strategic shift from a predominant counter-insurgency and stability operations period of warfare to preparing for higher-intensity, peer-to-peer conflict. It means as well that crisis management in a counter-insurgency operation is clearly different from those involving higher levels of conflict and potentially including peer competitors.

With the coming of the F-35, the Marines have led the way at the outset for the U.S. services which has meant that the Marines have been working closely with the USAF as that service brings its F-35s into initial operating capabilities. According to Col. Wellons: "We have always had a close relationship with the USN. We are after all Naval aviators. I cannot over-emphasize our close working relationship with the USN and Top Gun, where we have always had several USMC aviators filling highly sought-after exchange tours. We have some challenges but also many opportunities.

"Top Gun has a strong emphasis on Super Hornet and are just beginning to roll out their F-35C course, which we intend to support. We have legacy F/A-18s but do not fly the Super Hornet and the USMC has been leaning forward on the establishment of the full spectrum of F-35 tactics, having already executed five WTI classes with the F-35B.

"Recently we have made huge strides in establishing joint communications standards and we are closer now than ever before to aligning all the service standards with joint communications—all the service weapons schools have been cooperating in this effort. With regard to working with the USAF—over the past decade, as we operated together during the wars in Iraq and Afghanistan, we became much closer and better integrated across the service weapons schools.

"But the advent of the F-35 has really accelerated our close working relationship with the USAF. The standup of F-35 was "joint" from the very beginning, and the USMC has been aggressive with the stand up of our operational F-35s—the first of all the services to declare IOC, deploy overseas, and conduct weapons school courses with the F-35.

"As a result, we have been at the forefront of lessons-learned with the aircraft in terms of sustainment, deployability, expeditionary operations and tactical employment. We currently have a former USMC F/A-18 instructor pilot flying F-35As on an exchange tour with the USAF Weapons School, and we will soon have the first USAF F-35 exchange pilot coming to Yuma for a tour as instructor pilot in the F-35 division at MAWTS-1. We are all learning about employing, supporting and sustaining the F-35, and deploying it to places like the Western Pacific, where VMF-121 has been in place now a year."

Question: During my time in Australia earlier this year, the Commander of the 11th Air Force raised a key question about the need for the USAF to ramp up its mobile basing capabilities. How has the USAF interacted with the Marines at Yuma with regard to working through a new approach?

Col. Wellons: "Within the USMC, expeditionary operations are our bread and butter. In a contested environment, we will need to operate for hours at a base rather than weeks or months. At WTI we are working hard on mobile basing and, with the F-35, we are taking particular advantage of every opportunity to do distributed STOVL (Short Take-Off and Vertical Landing) operations. It is a work in progress but at the heart of our DNA. We will fly an Osprey or C-130 to a Forward Operating Base (FOB), bring in the F-35s, refuel them, and load them with weapons while the engines are still running, and then depart. In a very short period of time, we are taking off with a full load of fuel and weapons, and the Ospreys and/or C-130s follow close behind.

"We are constantly working on solutions to speed up the process, like faster fuel-flow rates, and hasty maintenance in such situations. Of course, we have operated off of ships with our F-35s from the beginning, and that is certainly an expeditionary basing platform.

"We have been pleased with what we have seen so far in regard to F-35 readiness at WTI. For example, in the last WTI class, we had six F-35s and we had five out of six up every day, which was certainly as good as anything we have seen with legacy aircraft. During the most recent class, F-35s supported us with over ninety-five sorties and a negligible cancellation rate. Our readiness rates at WTI are not representative of the fleet, where we continue to work on enhancing overall readiness goals with F-35."

We then discussed the F-35 and USMC operations beyond MAWTS-1.

Col. Wellons: "This is still an early variant of this airplane. It is the early days for the F-35 and we are working things like software evolution. Yet the aircraft has already had an impact in the PACOM AOR. We can put this airplane anywhere in the world, sustain it and fly it and get a key deterrent impact, as we have already begun to see."

Question: Looking back at your two and half years in command at MAWTS-1, what are some of your thoughts about the dynamics of change which you have seen while here?

Col. Wellons: "When I came here, the squadron was in great shape. I had the impression that what I needed to do was to focus on trying to sustain the standard of excellence that had already been established, because the squadron was really firing on all cylinders. I felt we were training at a world-class level and were training to the appropriate skills.

"But during my first year we faced dramatic and significant readiness challenges across Marine aviation, almost at an historic level. This led to significant reductions in the level of pilot proficiency and material readiness and challenged our ability to meet training objectives during WTI. The readiness cratering also impacted morale and placed our staff in a difficult position. If you have students that are coming to WTI that are barely qualified, who have just barely achieved the prerequisites necessary to come to a WTI class, that creates a risk management problem and makes it difficult to train at the graduate level"

"We were looking at dips in proficiency from flying fifteen to twenty hours a month down to ten or eleven hours a month or lower, and this required us to make some substantial adjustments to how we approached and ran the WTI class. Fortunately, this situation has dramatically changed for the better.

"During this last WTI course we had the highest level of readiness that I think we have ever seen for our fixed wing fleet, and our pilots are back above twenty hours a month across all communities. I would caution that we view this readiness recovery as fragile at this point, but it is definitely headed in the right direction."

Question: Clearly, there is a strategic shift underway for U.S. and allied forces to now operate in contested environments. That has happened during your time here. How has that affected what you have had MAWTS-1 focus upon?

Col. Wellons: "The team at 29 Palms as well as at Yuma have ramped up the contested and degraded environment that we present to our training audience at WTI and across all the other service level MAGTF training venues. We have challenged our students, especially this year, to operate in environments where communications and navigation systems are challenged, facing the most sophisticated and capable adversaries we can find. We focused on the idea that in the future fight our primary means of navigation and communication will probably be denied, and certainly degraded and our operators may have to use old fashioned techniques to get bombs on target."

Question: You are clearly working what might be called F-35 2.0 while flushing out the dynamics of 1.0. And one key area where that is

happening is with regard to the sensor-shooter relationship. We talked last year about this dynamic, what has been happening since then?[14]

Col. Wellons: "In part, it is about the transformation of the amphibious fleet whereby the shipboard strike systems or sensor systems can work with the reach of the F-35 as a fleet. For example, we see clear interest from the Navy's side in exploiting fifth-generation capabilities in the amphibious fleet using the Up-Gunned Expeditionary Strike Group (ESG), that will better leverage the capability they have got with the F-35.

"Naval integration will be a major line of effort in the WTI course going forward. The F-35 is leading to a fundamental reworking of where we can take the sensor-shooter relationship. We tend to focus on the airplane's sensor and how that sensor can go out and find a target and employ its own ordinance on that target. That is certainly something which the F-35 can do.

"But it can also enable an off-board shot, as in the case of High Mobility Artillery Rocket system or HIMARS/F-35 integration. Or it can work with the G/ATOR radar on the ship or the ground to enable weapons solutions for other platforms in the distributed battlespace. It then becomes a question of how I maximize the number of targets I can hit with the F-35 distributed force rather than how many targets can an individual fighter hit. This is part of the combat learning we are working on at MAWTS-1 as well."

Question: Assuming readiness remains at an appropriate level, what challenges do you see in the near term with regard to training?

Col. Wellons: "Clearly, a major challenge we face is the limitations of our training ranges. We need to expand the potential of tasks we can do on these ranges to replicate a realistic and lethal contested environment. This is another consequence of our budget challenges in recent years, and we are pushing hard for upgrades of all our emitters, target sets, and simulation capability in order to enable full spectrum training at the high end."

---

14   "F-35 2.0: Introducing the Concept," *Second Line of Defense*, 2018, https://sldinfo.com/2018/09/f-35-2-o-introducing-the-concept/.

Col. Gillette, CO of MAWTS-1, 2020

September 22, 2020

Prior to my visit in early September 2020, I conducted a series of tele-conferences with MAWTS-1 officers in the late Spring and early Summer. The focus of those discussions was upon mobile and expeditionary basing and how the training for this key capability was being shaped going forward for the Marines.

During this visit, I had a chance to engage with a number of MAWTS-1 officers and with the CO of MAWTS-1, Colonel Gillette, with regard to the focus and training with regard to the USMC's emphasis on their contribution to naval warfare.

Question: How is the Marine Corps going to contribute most effectively to the Pacific mission in terms of Sea Control and Sea Denial? And how to best contribute to the defensive and offensive operations affecting the SLOCs? And I think both questions highlight the challenge of shaping a force with enough flexibility to have pieces on the chessboard and to move them effectively to shape combat success.

Col. Gillette: "Working through how the USMC can contribute effectively to sea control and sea denial for the joint force is a key challenge. The way I see it, is the question of how to insert force in the Pacific where a key combat capability is to bring assets to bear on the Pacific chessboard. The long-precision weapons of adversaries are working to expand their reach and shape an opportunity to work multiple ways inside and outside those strike zones to shape the battlespace.

"What do we need to do in order to bring our assets inside the red rings our adversaries are seeking to place on the Pacific chessboard? How do you bring your chess pieces onto the board in a way that ensures or minimizes both the risk to the force and enhances the probability of a positive outcome for the mission? How do you move assets on the chessboard inside those red rings which allows us to bring capabilities to bear on whatever end state we are trying to achieve?

"For the USMC, as the Commandant has highlighted, it is a question of how we can most effectively contribute to the air-maritime fight. For us, a core competence is mobile basing which clearly will play a key part in our contribution, whether projected from afloat or ashore. What assets need to be on the chessboard at the start of any type of escalation? What assets need to be brought to bear and how do you bring them there? I think mobile basing is part of the discussion of how you bring those forces to bear.

"How do you bring forces afloat inside the red rings in a responsible way so that you can bring those pieces to the chessboard or have them contribute to the overall crisis management objectives? How do we escalate and de-escalate force to support our political objectives? How do we, either from afloat or ashore, enable the joint force to bring relevant assets to bear on the crisis and then once we establish that force presence, how do we manage it most effectively? How do we train to be able to do that? What integration in the training environment is required to be able to achieve such an outcome in an operational setting in a very timely manner?"

Question: Ever since the revival of the Bold Alligator exercises, I have focused on how the amphibious fleet can shift form its greyhound bus role to shaping a task force capable of operating in terms of sea denial and sea control. With the new America-class ships in the fleet, this clearly is the case. How do you view the revamping of the amphibious fleet in terms of providing new for the USMC and the U.S. Navy to deliver sea control and sea denial?[15]

Col. Gillette: "The traditional approach for the amphibious force is to move force to an area of interest. Now we need to look at the entire maritime combat space, and ask how we can contribute to that combat space, and not simply move force from A to B.

"I think the first leap is to think of the amphibious task force, as you call it, to become a key as pieces on the chessboard. As with any piece, they

---

15 "Shaping the Single Naval Battle: Bold Alligator 2013 and the Way Ahead," *Second Line of Defense*, June 2013, https://sldinfo.com/wp-content/uploads/2013/06/Bold-Alligator-2013-Special-Report-1.pdf.

have strengths and weaknesses. Some of the weaknesses are clear, such as the need for a common operational picture, a command and control suite to where the assets that provide data feeds to a carrier strike group are also incorporated onto L-Class shipping. We're working on those things right now, in order to bring the SA of those types of ships up to speed with the rest of the Naval fleet."

Question: A key opportunity facing the force is to reimagine how to use the assets the force has now but working them in new innovative integratable ways or, in other words, rethinking how to use assets that we already have but differently. How do you view this opportunity?

Col. Gillette: "We clearly need to focus on the critical gaps which are evident from working a more integrated force. I think that the first step is to reimagine what pieces can be moved around the board for functions that typically in the past haven't been used in the new way.

"That's number one. Number two, once you say, "Okay, well I have all these LHA/LHD class shipping and all the LPDs et cetera that go along with the traditional MEU-R, is there a ship that I need to either tether to that MEU-R to give it a critical capability that's autonomous? Or do I just need to have a way to send data so that they have the same sensing of the environment that they're operating in, using sensors already in the carrier strike group, national assets, Air Force assets et cetera?"

"In other words, the ship might not have to be tethered to a narrowly defined task force but you just need to be able to have the information that everybody else does so that you can make tactical or operational decisions to employ that ship to the max extent practical of its capabilities.

"There is a significant shift underway. The question we are now posing is, What capability do I need, and can I get it from a sister service that already has something that provides the weapons, the C2 or the ISR that I need? I need to know how to exploit information which benefits either my SA, my offensive or defensive capability of my organic force. But you don't necessarily need to own it in order to benefit from it.

"And I think that when we really start talking about integration, that's probably one of the things that we could realize very quickly is that there are certain, assets, and data streams that come from the Air Force or the Navy that make the USMC a more lethal and effective force, and vice versa.

"The key question becomes: How do I get the most decisive information into an LHA/LHD? How do I get it into a marine unit so that they can benefit from that information and then act more efficiently or lethally when required?"

Question: We first met when you were at Eglin where you were working the F-35 warfare system into the USMC. Now that the F-35s are becoming a fact of life for both the U.S. services and the allies in the Pacific, how can we best leverage that integratable capability?

Col. Gillette: "The development is a significant one. It is not only a question of interoperability among the F-35 fleet, it is the ability to have common logistical and support in the region with your allies, flying the same aircraft with the same parts. And the big opportunity comes with regard to the information point I made earlier. We are in the early stages of exploiting what the F-35 force can provide in terms of information dominance in the Pacific, but the foundation has been laid.

"And when we highlight the F-35 as the twenty-first-century version of what the World War II Navy called the big blue blanket with the redundancy and the amount of information that could be utilized, it's pretty astonishing if you think about it.

"The challenge is to work the best ways to sort through the information resident in the F-35 force and then how do you utilize it in an effective and efficient way for the joint force. But the foundation is clearly there."

Question: Clearly, the new focus on the maritime battle requires a shift in USMC training. How are you approaching that challenge?

Col. Gillette: "So long as I've been in the Marine Corps and the way that it still currently is today, marine aviation exists to support the ground combat. That's why we exist. The idea that we travel light and that the aviation element within the MAGTAF provides or helps to provide the ground combat element with a significant capability is our legacy.

"We are now taking that legacy and adapting it. We are taking the traditional combat engagement where you have battalions maneuvering and aviation supporting that ground element and we are moving it toward Sea Control, and Sea Denial missions.

"We are reimagining the potential of what the infantry does. That doesn't mean that they do that exclusively because, although I think that our focus in the Marine Corps, as the Commandant said, is shifting toward the Pacific that doesn't relegate or negate the requirement to be ready to respond to all of the other things that the Marine Corps does. It might be less of a focus, but I don't think that that negates our requirement to deal with a variety of core missions.

"It's a question of working the balance in the training continuum. What does an infantry battalion train to? Do they train to a more traditional battalion in the attack or in the defense and then how do I use my aviation assets to support either one of those types of operations?" As opposed to, "I might have to take an island, a piece of territory that we're going to use a mobile base, secure it so that we can continue to push chess pieces forward in the Pacific, in the Sea Control, Sea Denial end-state."

"Those are two very different kind of skill sets. If there's one thing that the Marine Corps is very good at it's being very versatile and being able to switch from one to the other on relatively short order. But in order to do that, you have to have a very dedicated and well thought-out training continuum so that people can do both well, because if you say that you can do it, the expectation is that you can do it well.

"We are shaping a new Marine Littoral Regiment, MLR, but we're still in the nascent stages of defining what are the critical tasks that something like that needs to be able to do and then how you train to it. How do we create not only the definition of the skill sets that we need to train large formations to, but then what venues must we have to train? How to best combine simulated environments with real world training out on a range?

"We're working through all that right now and it'll be interesting to watch how that process unfolds, but it is definitely a mind shift to rethink the context in which our Ground Combat Element will conduct offensive of defensive operations, and specifically, what tasks they are expected to be capable of in this environment."

"What we've done in the past is very well-defined, and we have a very defined training continuum for those large formations. In this new role in the Pacific, that's something that I think over the next few years we'll get our arms around and we will learn from doing. As we start to field these formations out to the Pacific, we'll really start to figure out where are we good at training and where are gaps that we need to close and shape the venues and methods to fill those in those gaps.

"We're constantly looking at new venues and new methods to start to do the things that we need to do with the new approach. For example, we are taking our TACAIR Community up to the Nellis range for large integrated strike missions. We do face-to-face planning with the Air Force and Navy so that our students can understand the capabilities and limitations of these different platforms. They rub elbows with the USAF and USN operators and gain first-hand knowledge of the strengths and weaknesses of these different platforms.

"Then we fly them all back home and then the next night we go out with this huge armada of joint assets. Out of the assets that play on this, it's probably 50 percent Marines and the other 50 percent are Growlers, Air Force platforms et cetera. And then we do a mass debrief.

"And this starts to chip away at the legacy perspective: "Okay, I'm a master of my machine." They come to WTI and learn how to think an integrated manner. But more importantly, they get exposed and actually go out and do the integration with joint service assets to see the strengths and weaknesses so that they understand the planning considerations required for the joint fight against peer competitors and how to work beyond what their Marine Corps platform can do.

"Another example is when we do what we call our Offensive Anti-Air Warfare, OAAW Evolution. We fight peer versus peer against one another. We have real-time intelligent collects on what the other side is doing, so the plans change real-time, airborne and on the ground. There's deception; there's decoys. It's pretty amazing to watch and oh, by the way, they get to use their weapons systems, their command and control systems to the fullest extent of their capabilities on both sides. This allows us to engage a thinking, breathing enemy who is well-trained and has all the latest and greatest systems, but they do that with assets that not are resident just to the Marine Corps.

"We operate with assets that come from the Department of Defense to show them the importance, on both sides, whether it's the C2 with their surface-to-air missiles and their own red fighters or the blue fighters with both organic assets, as well as national assets.

"We are focused on operating, not just with the assets that you control, the ones that sit out on our flight line or sit in our command and control, but how these other things can contribute in the joint fight. And to shape effective methods to get the enabling information, digest it and then use it in near real-time.

"It's pretty interesting to watch and the outcomes of this evolution are wildly different, based on the ability of the students to use these things that they're not used to working with, incorporate them in real-time into their plan and then execute. I think, if you were to look at any high-end conflict or contingency where you have similarly matched forces in terms of training and gear, it would be similar. That will make the difference between somebody who is wildly successful or wildly unsuccessful, with your ability to direct and use those things real-time being a crucial delineator to combat success."

Question: How do you see the growth of simulation in this training approach?

Col. Gillette: "You can never just say, "I'm going to train only in a simulated environment." The simulated environment is good for a number of reasons. One key contribution is your ability to connect simulators, pick whatever platform it is.

"We are working with the surface warfare elements of the USN to incorporate synthetic/real training. What that will enable us to do is, take live fly events with their simulator event and start to fuse those two worlds, the simulated world as well as the live fly. And this allows us to create, not only a complex, robust environment that has airplanes, real airplanes, synthetic airplanes, synthetic ships, both good and bad, but then go out to try and then solve a problem in that environment.

"We're just starting to put our big toe into this new environment, but I think what we will find is that a surface warfare officer can learn how a F-35 might sense something that they would then prioritize high enough that they would want to shoot with one of their organic weapons.

"If I could I'd have every joint asset come to our WTI exercise, every class and integrate with our people. The reality is, due to real-world realties, these high-demand, low-density assets will often not be free to come.

"However, if I could create a simulated environment where I could get reps from an F-35 perspective, from a Viper, it doesn't matter what platform it is, but they get used to thinking about receiving and then executing off the information that would come from one of those high-demand, low-density assets. I think what it will do is make our ability to then plug and play in a future contingency.

"Another piece of the puzzle is to determine: how do we go from the simulator to a blending of live event with some amount of simulation mixed in there to create the contested environment?

"And a lot of people define what is a contested environment differently, but what you'll be able to do is to create an environment which you actually go fly in, from Marine Aviation's perspective, against a threat that's both real and simulated.

"We will shape a blended training environment as opposed to, "I do simulators and then I try to replicate it as best I can out on the range with real things." There'll be requirements to have real things out on the range but there will be a blending, which, from the operator's perspective, it will be no different than a completely live environment."

Working Mobile Basing

May 31, 2020

The USMC has mobile basing in its DNA. With the strategic shift from the Middle Eastern land wars to full spectrum crisis management, an ability to distribute a force but to do so with capabilities which allow it to be integratable is crucial.

For the Marines, this means an ability to operate an integratable force from seabases, forward operating bases (FOBs) or FARPs. As the Marines look forward to the decade ahead, they are likely to enhance their capabilities to provide for mobile bases which can empower the joint and coalition force by functioning as a chess piece on the kill web enabled chessboard.

But what is required to do mobile basing? What are the baseline requirements to be successful?

A very good place to start to shape answers to these questions is to be found at the USMC's center of excellence on warfighting training, MAWTS-1 located at MCAS Yuma. In a recent discussion with Lt. Colonel Barron, ADT&E Department Head at MAWTS-1, we did just that. ADT&E is not only focused on the core task of fighting today with the current force but also looking forward to how to enhance that force's capabilities in the near to mid-term as well.

We had a wide-ranging discussion with regard to the flexible basing dynamic. The discussion with Lt. Col. Barton highlighted six key takeaways. The first one is the crucial need for decision makers to determine why a mobile base is being generated and what the tactical or strategic purpose of doing so is. It takes time and effort to create a mobile base, and the mobile base commander will need to operate with mission command with regard to his base to determine how best to operate and for what purpose.

The second one is the importance of determining the projected duration of the particular base. This will have a significant impact in shaping the question of logistics support. What is needed? How to get it there? And from what supply depot, afloat, or ashore in adjacent areas?

The third one is clearly the question of inserting the force into the mobile base and ensuring its optimal capabilities for survivability. What needs to be at the base to provide for organic survivability? What cross links via C2 and ISR will provide for an extended kill web to support the base and its survivability?

A fourth one is to determine what the base needs to do to contribute to the wider joint or coalition force. With the evolution of technology, it is possible now to have processing power, and strike capabilities distributed and operated by a smaller logistics footprint force, but how best to configure that base to provide the desired combat effect for the joint or coalition force?

A fifth one is clearly a crucial one for operating in a contested environment. Here the need is for signature control, or an ability to have as small a signature footprint as possible commensurate with achieving the desired combat effect. Signature management could be seen as a component of survivability. However, the management of signatures down to the small unit level requires a significant focus of attention and effort.

The sixth one is clearly having an exit strategy in mind. For how long should the force be at the mobile base? For what purposes? And what needs to be achieved to enable the decision to move from the mobile base?

In effect, the discussion highlighted what one might refer to as the three Ss. An insertion force operating from a variety of mobile bases needs to be able to be sustainable, survivable, and signature manageable.

With regard to current USMC capabilities, the MV-22, the C-130, the Viper, the Venom, the CH-53E, and the F-35 are the key platforms, which allow the Marines to integrate and move a lethal combat force to a mobile base. But the C2/ISR enablement is a key part of the requirement and the digital interoperability (DI) efforts are a key part of shaping a more effective way ahead. And in the relatively near term, the Ch-53K replacing the E is a key enabler for an enhanced mobile basing strategy.

It is clear as well as the U.S. services work their way ahead in the evolving strategic environment, that the USMC core skill set with mobile basing will figure more prominently, and become a key part of the Marines working with the joint and coalition force in shaping a more effective way ahead for the operation of the integrated distributed force.

Moving Forward with Mobile Basing

June 3, 2020

As noted earlier, a key contribution which the USMC can provide for the joint and coalition force either afloat or ashore is mobile and expeditionary basing. It is clear that as the joint and coalition force shapes greater capabilities through C2/ISR innovations and integrability of the sensor-strike kill web, that capabilities will be enhanced to operate distributed expeditionary basing for the insertion forces.

But one fights with the force one has and builds forward from there. So where are the Marines currently with regard to mobile basing capabilities? In the discussion with Major Brian Hansell, MAWTS-1 F-35 Division Head, it is clear that the coming of the F-35 to the USMC has expanded their ability to operate within a broader kill web and to both empower their expeditionary bases as well as to contribute to the broader kill web approach. The Marine's F-35s are part of the broader joint and coalition force of F-35s, and notably in the Pacific this extends the reach significantly of the Marine's F-35s and brings greater SA as well as reach to other strike platforms to the force operating from an expeditionary base as well as enhancing the kill web reach for the joint or coalition force. As Major Hansell put it: "By being an expeditionary, forward-based service, we're effectively extending the bounds of the kill web for the entire joint and coalition force."

The F-35 brings a unique capability to the Marine Corps as it works mobile basing but reworking the assault force more generally is a work in progress. The DI initiative is a crucial one as the assault assets will have integrability they do not currently have, such as the Viper attack helicopter getting Link-16.

And the heavy lift element, the CH-53E, which is a bedrock capability for the insertion force, is older, not easily integratable, and is in diminishing numbers. The CH-53K which is to replace it will provide significant capability enhancements for an insertion force operating from afloat or ashore mobile bases but needs to be ramped up in numbers capable of raising the combat level of the current force.

In a discussion with Major James Everett, head of the Assault Support Department at MAWTS-1, we discussed the force that we have and some ways ahead for enhanced capability in the near to mid-term. The Assault Support Department includes a number of key divisions: CH-53, MV-22, KC-130, UH-1, and AH-1.

The first takeaway from our discussion was that indeed we need to focus on the force we have now, because we will fight with the force we have now. The Marines by being in the land wars for the past twenty years, have become part of the joint force, and have relied on elements from the joint force, that they would not necessarily have access to when doing force insertion in the Pacific.

This means that the DI effort under way within Marine Corps innovation is not just a nice to have effort, but a crucial one to ensure that the insertion force package can work more effectively together and to leverage other key support assets which might be available from the joint or coalition force. After all, a mobile base is being put on the chessboard for a strategic or tactical objective and survivability is a key requirement.[16]

The second point is about sustainability. And sustainability is a function of the lift assets which can bring the kit and supplies needed for the duration of the mission. For the Marines, this is defined by KC-130J, CH-53E, MV-22, and UH-1Y lift support. And it is also defined by air refuellable assets to the assault force as well. The Marines have limited indigenous assets to provide aerial refueling which, dependent on the mission and the time scale

---

16 "The USMC's Digital Interoperability Initiative and Effort," *Defense.info* (April 2020)., https://defense.info/highlight-of-the-week/usmcs-digital-interoperability-initiative-and-effort/.

of the force insertion effort, might need to depend on the Navy or Air Force for this capability.

The third point is about C2. With the shift from the land wars, where the Marines were embedded within CENTCOM forces, C2 was very hierarchical. This clearly is not going to be practicable or efficacious with a distributed insertion force. Working mission command for a force operating in a degraded environment is a key challenge, but one which will have to be met to deliver the kind of distributed mobile-based force which the Marines can provide for the joint and coalition force, and not just only in the Pacific, but would certainly provide a significant capability as well for the fourth battle of the Atlantic.

The fourth point is the clear importance of the coming of the CH-53K to the force. It is not only a question of a modern lift asset with significantly enhanced capabilities to provide for assault support, it is that it is a digital aircraft which can fully participate in an integrated distributed mission set.

The fifth point is that the digital interoperable initiative will not only provide for ways to better integrate assets but also enhance what those assets can do. A key example is the nature of what a Viper assault asset can do afloat as well ashore when operating with Link-16 and full motion video.

The sixth point is that the coming of remotes whether air or maritime can expand the SA of the insertion force, as long as signatures can be managed effectively. And for the insertion force this can be about remotes transported to a base, operating from an afloat asset, or tapping into various overhead assets, such as Triton.

Or put another way, as DI is worked, there will be expanded effort to find ways to support the insertion force operating from a mobile base. This will be an interactive process between what C2/ISR assets are available in the kill web, and how the Marines ashore or afloat can best use those resources. We have seen such a migration with the USN as the CSG and fleet is adding MISR or Maritime ISR officers, and this change actually was inspired by the operations of third MEF in Afghanistan. What we might envisage is simply the next iteration of what was done ashore with now the afloat and insertion forces in the maritime environment.

The seventh point is the key emphasis on timeliness for a mobile basing option. It is about the insertion force operating within the adversary's decision cycle and operating to get the desired combat effect prior to that adversary being successful in getting his combat result, namely, eliminating or degrading the insertion force. This is another way to understand the key significance of how C2/ISR is worked between the insertion force and the wider air–maritime force.

In short, the Marines will fight with the force they have; and as far as near term modernization, ensuring that DI is built in and accelerated, full use of what an F-35 wolfpack can bring to the insertion force, and the continuing modernization of the assault force staring with the coming of the CH-53K in sufficient numbers, these are all key ways ahead. And as the C2/ISR kill webs are built out and remotes folded into these kill webs, force insertion via mobile basing will clearly be enhanced as well.

The Role of Heavy Lift

September 21, 2020

During my discussions earlier this year with a number of MAWTS-1 officers, we focused on the thinking and training of the USMC to further enhance their capabilities for mobile and expeditionary basing. Obviously, the insertion of force into a flexible basing environment requires lift capabilities, and with rapid insertion, movement and withdrawal of force being a key enabler for able to work an effective basing chessboard, heavy lift is a key enabler.

And heavy lift really comes in two forms: fixed wing aircraft and rotorcraft. My guide in the discussion of the lift-basing dynamic earlier this year was Major James Everett, head of the Assault Support Department at MAWTS-1. In that discussion, we focused on the importance of the CH-53E and the new aircraft, the CH-53K in enabling mobile and expeditionary basing.

In September 2020, we met at MAWTS-1 to continue our discussion.

But the focus of my visit was on addressing the challenges the Marines face in supporting the USN in terms of the maritime fight. In particular, my discussions with Colonel Gillette, the CO of MAWTS-1 focused on two key questions: "How is the Marine Corps going to contribute most effectively to the Pacific mission in terms of Sea Control and Sea Denial? And how to best contribute to the defensive and offensive operations affecting the SLOCs?

We addressed how to answer these questions from the standpoint of the assault support force. As Major Everett put it: "a key focus of effort for the assault support community is upon how we can best assist through expeditionary basing to provide for sea control. We're trying to get away from any permanent type of land basing in a maritime contested environment."

A key enabler for flexible basing inserts or operations from the maritime fleet, inclusive of the amphibious ships, are the capabilities which the Marine Corps has with its tiltrotor and rotorcraft community. This community provides an ability to insert a sizable force without the need for airstrips of the size which a KC-130J would need. Or put in another way, the Marines can look at basing options and sustainability via air either in terms of basing options where a fixed wing aircraft must operate, or, in a much wider set of cases, where vertical lift assets can operate.

The third is obviously by sea, which depends on support by a mother ship or a Military Sealift Command (MSC) ship, but the challenge for the Marines is that moving bases deeper into the maritime area of operations creates enhanced challenges for the MSC and raises questions about viable sustainable options. We have already seen this challenge with regard to the littoral combat ship fleet, where the MSC is not eager to move into the littorals to supply a smaller ship, but it is much more willing to take its ships into a task force environment with significant maritime strike capability to give it protection.[17]

---

17   For our most recent MSC interview, see the following: Robbin Laird, "Sustaining the Integrated Distributed Force at Sea: The Military Sealift Command Challenge," *Second Line of Defense* (December 9, 2020).

The most flexibility for the mobile or expeditionary basing options clearly comes from vertical lift support aircraft. The challenge is that the current CH-53E fleet has been heavily tasked by the more than a decade of significant engagement in the Middle East. The Marines unlike the U.S. Army did not bring back their heavy lift helicopters for deep maintenance but focused on remaining engaged in the fight by doing the just enough maintenance to continue safe and effective flight operations in theater.

As Major Everett put it: "The Army brought their helicopters back from Afghanistan and they'd strip them down to the frame and they'd rebuild them basically. We just didn't do that." This means that the heavy lift operational force inventory is relatively low compared to the required capabilities.

And as the focus shifts to the Pacific, with its tyranny of distance and the brutal operating conditions often seen in the maritime domain, having a very robust airlift fleet becomes not a nice to have, but a foundational element. The replacement for the E, the CH-53K, will provide a significant enhancement to the lift capability, and sustainability in operations as well.

It is also a question of being able to deliver combat support speed or CSS to the mobile or expeditionary base, and clearly the combination of tiltrotor and heavy lift can do that.

But the challenge will be having adequate numbers of such assets, notably, because the nature of the environment is very challenging, and the operational demand will go up significantly if one wants to operate a distributed force but one which is sustained and protected by an integrated force. As Major Everett put it: "There's no way with the types of shipping and numbers of shipping we have, that we could possibly carry enough aircraft on that shipping to enable any type of land control without 53s."

An aspect that makes the upgraded heavy lift fleet a key enabler for expeditionary basing will be the installation of a mesh network manager into the digital cockpit of the CH-53K, and its build into the legacy aircraft as well. This makes it part of an integratable force, not just an island presence force. As Major Everett put it: "The core kind of skills that fifty-three pilots train to, are not going to change. But obviously the physicality of the new helicopter is very different. It can lift more relevant materials or assets and in larger numbers. It holds the 463L pallets that allow for rapid off and on-loads from the fixed wing aircraft which could provide distribution points for the heavy lift fleet. Additionally, the impact of the CH-53K's integrated DI and its integration into the kill web will be significant."

In short, the desire to have a Marine Corps enhanced role in sea control and sea denial with an island strategy really enhances the importance of heavy lift helicopters.

Forward Arming and Refueling Points (FARPs)

June 8, 2020

When considering contributions which the USMC can make to the joint or coalition force in Pacific operations, an ability to put an air arming and refueling point on virtually any spot on the kill web chessboard is clearly a key contribution. These are referred to as FARPs or Forward Arming and Refueling Points but are really Arming and Refueling Points because where one might put them on the chessboard depends on how one wants to support the task forces within a kill web.

In looking at a theater of operations, and certainly one with the tyranny of distance of the Pacific, one needs to be able to have a layer of fuel support for operations. For the Marines operating from the sea, this clearly includes combat ships, MSC tankers and related ships, as well as airborne tanker assets. By deploying a relatively small logistics footprint FARP or ARP, one can provide a much wider of points to provide fuel for the combat force. And in Marine terms, the size of that footprint will depend on whether that FARP is enabled by KC-130J support or by CH-53E support, with both air assets requiring significantly different basing to work the FARP.

I discussed FARP operations and ways to rework those operations going forward with Maj Steve Bancroft, Aviation Ground Support (AGS) Department Head, MAWTS-1, MCAS Yuma. There were a number of takeaways from that conversation which provide an understanding of how the Marines are working their way ahead currently with regard to the FARP contribution to distributed operations.

The first takeaway is that when one is referring to a FARP, it is about an ability to provide a node which can refuel and rearm aircraft. But it is more than that. It is about providing capability for crew rest, resupply and repair to some extent.

The second takeaway is that the concept remains the same, but the tools to do the concept are changing. Clearly, one example is the nature of the fuel containers being used. In the land wars, the basic fuel supply was being carried by a fuel truck to the FARP location. Obviously, that is not a solution for Pacific operations. What is being worked now at MAWTS-1 is a much mobile solution set. Currently, they are working with a system whose provenance goes back to the 1950s and is a helicopter expeditionary refueling system or HERS system. This legacy kit limits mobility as it is very heavy and requires the use of several hoses and fuel separators.

Obviously, this solution is too limiting so they are working a new solution set. They are testing a mobile refueling asset called TAGRS or a Tactical Aviation Ground Refueling system.

The third takeaway was that even with a more mobile and agile pumping solution, there remains the basic challenge of the weight of fuel as a commodity. A gallon of gas is about 6.7 pounds and when aggregating enough fuel at a FARP, the challenge is how to get adequate supplies to a FARP for its mission to be successful. To speed up the process, the Marines are experimenting with more disposable supply containers to provide for enhanced speed of movement among FARPs within an extended battlespace. They have used helos and KC-130Js to drop pallets of fuel as one solution to this problem.

The effort to speed up the creation and withdrawal from FARPs is a task being worked by the Marines at MAWTS-1 as well. In effect, they are working a more disciplined cycle of arrival and departure from FARPs. And the Marines are exercising ways to bring in a FARP support team in a single aircraft to further the logistical footprint and to provide for more rapid engagement and disengagement as well.

The fourth takeaway is that innovative delivery solutions can be worked going forward. When I met in early 2020 with Col. Perrin, Program Manager, PMA-261 H53 Heavy Lift Helicopters, U.S. Naval Air Systems Command at Pax River Naval Air Station, we discussed how the CH-53K as a smart aircraft could manage airborne MULES to support resupply to a mobile base. As Col. Perrin noted in our conversation: "The USMC has done many studies of distributed operations, and throughout the analyses, it is clear that heavy lift is an essential piece of the ability to do such operations."[18] And not just any heavy lift—but heavy lift built around a digital architecture.

Clearly, the CH-53E being more than thirty years old is not built in such a manner, but the CH-53K is. What this means is that the CH-53K "can operate and fight on the digital battlefield."

And because the flight crew are enabled by the digital systems onboard, they can focus on the mission rather than focusing primarily on the mechanics of flying the aircraft. This will be crucial as the Marines shift to using unmanned systems more broadly than they do now.

For example, it is clearly a conceivable future that CH-53Ks would be flying a heavy lift operation with unmanned "mules" accompanying them. Such manned-unmanned teaming requires a lot of digital capability and bandwidth, a capability built into the CH-53K.

If one envisages the operational environment in distributed terms, this means that various types of sea bases, ranging from large deck carriers to various types of Maritime Sealift Command ships, along with expeditionary bases, or FARPs or FOBS, will need to be connected into a combined combat force.

---

18   Robbin Laird, "Colonel Jack Perrin on the CH-53K Program: An Update," *Defense. info* (February 25, 2020), https://defense.info/interview-of-the-week/colonel-jack-perrin-on-the-ch-53k-program-an-update-on-a-key-program/

To establish expeditionary bases, it is crucial to be able to set them up, operate, and to leave such a base rapidly or in an expeditionary manner (sorry for the pun). This will be virtually impossible to do without heavy lift, and vertical heavy lift, specifically. Put in other terms, the new strategic environment requires new operating concepts; and in those operating concepts, the CH-53K provides significant requisite capabilities. So why not the possibility of the CH-53K flying in with a couple of MULES which carried fuel containers; or perhaps building a vehicle which could come off of the cargo area of the CH-53K and move on the operational area and be linked up with TAGRS?

If distributed FARPs are an important contribution to the joint and coalition forces, then it will certainly be the case that "autonomous" systems will play a role in the evolution of the concept and provide some of those new tools which Maj. Bancroft highlighted.

MAWTS-1 and the F-35

May 29, 2020

Over the past few weeks, I have been discussing with USAF and USN officers, how the two services are training to shape greater synergy with regard to the integrated distributed force.

The fusing of multiple sensors via a common interactive self-healing web enhances the ability of the entire force, including key partners and allies, to engage cooperatively enemy targets in a time of conflict. Interactive webs can be used for a wide range of purposes throughout the spectrum of conflict and are a key foundation for full spectrum crisis management. To play their critical role when it comes to strike, whether kinetic or non-kinetic, this final layer of the web needs to have the highest standards of protection possible.

From the USAF and USN perspective, where does the USMC fit into the evolving kill web approach? Clearly, one answer which has been given several times can be expressed in terms of one of the Marines key competence—bringing an integrated force to a mobile operational setting whether afloat or ashore. It is important to consider a base afloat or ashore as part of the chessboard from a basing point of view. Too often when one mentions basing, the mind goes quickly to a fixed air or ground base, but in the evolving strategic environment, an ability to work across a wide variety of basing options is crucial.

And no force in the world is more focused on how to do this than the USMC. With the arrival of the *USS America* class LHA, the amphibious fleet moves out from its greyhound bus role to being able to contribute fully to sea control in transit or in operations, thereby relieving the USN large deck carriers from a primary protection role. To be clear, when one is talking about a combat cloud, the processing power empowering webs comes from cloud processing power. With a focus on interactive kill webs, the processing power is distributed.

The capability of the F-35s to hunt as a pack and through its CNI system and data fusion capabilities, the pack can work as one. The integration of the F-35 into the Marine Corps and its ability to work with joint and coalition F-35s provides significant reach to F-35 empowered mobile bases afloat or ashore.

In a discussion prior to the September 2020 visit to MAWTS-1 with Major Brian "Flubes" Hansell, MAWTS-1 F-35 Division Head, we focused on how the Marines are working the F-35 into their approach or better yet approaches to expeditionary basing

The first takeaway from that conversation is that following a significant focus on the land wars in the past twenty years combined with the return to the sea, the Marines are shaping new capabilities to operate at sea and in a way that can have significant combat effects on the expanded battlespace. And they are doing so from expeditionary bases, afloat and ashore. According to Major Hansell: "The Marine Corps is a force committed to expeditionary operations. When it comes to F-35, we are focused on how best to operate the F-35 in the evolving expeditionary environment, and I think we are pushing the envelope more than other services and other partners in this regard. One of the reasons we are able to do this is because of our organizational culture. If you look at the history of the Marine Corps, that's what we do. We are an expeditionary, forward-leaning service that prides itself in flexibility and adaptability."

The second takeaway is that the coming of the F-35 to the USMC has expanded their ability to operate within a broader kill web and to both empower their expeditionary bases as well as to contribute to the broader kill web approach. The Marine's F-35s are part of the broader joint and coalition force of F-35s, and notably in the Pacific this extends the reach significantly of the Marine's F-35s and brings greater SA as well as reach to other strike platforms to the force operating from an expeditionary base as well as enhancing the kill web reach for the joint or coalition force.

On the one hand, the F-35 leads the wolfpack. This was a concept which Secretary Wynne highlighted when I worked for him in DoD. His perspective then is now reality and one which empowers an expeditionary force. Simply put, the F-35 does not tactically operate as a single aircraft. It hunts as a network-enabled, cooperative four-ship fighting a fused picture and was designed to do so from the very beginning. "We hunt as a pack. Future upgrades may look to expand the size of the pack." Indeed, in the most recent software block, the size of the pack has been expanded to eight F-35s.

The hunt concept and the configuration of the wolfpack is important not just in terms of understanding how the wolfpack can empower the ground insertion force with a mobile kill web capability but also in terms of the configuration of aircraft on the sea base working both sea control and support to what then becomes a land base insertion force.

The fourth takeaway focuses on the reach not range point about the F-35 global enterprise. A USMC F-35 wolfpack has reach through its unique C2 and data fusion links into other U.S. service or coalition force F-35s with which it can link and work. And given the global enterprise, the coalition and joint partners are working seamlessly because of common TTP. As Major Hansell put it: "From the very beginning we write a tactics manual that is distributed to every country that buys the F-35. This means that if I need to integrate with a coalition F-35 partner, I know they understand how to employ this aircraft, because they're studying and practicing and training in the same manner that we are. And because we know how to integrate so well, we can distribute well in the extended battlespace as well. I'm completely integrated with the allied force into one seamless kill web via the F-35 as a global force enabler."

The fifth takeaway is the evolving role of the amphibious task force in the sea control mission. With the changing capabilities of strategic adversaries, sea control cannot be assumed but must be established. With the coming of the F-35 to the amphibious force, the role of that force in sea control is expanding and when worked with large deck carriers can expand the capabilities of the afloat force's ability to establish and exercise sea control.

With the coming of the *USS America* Class LHA, the large deck amphibious ship with its F-35s onboard is no longer a greyhound bus, but a significant contributor to sea control as well. As Major Hansell noted: "The LHA and LHD can plug and play into the sea control concept. It's absolutely something you would want if your mission is sea control. There is tremendous flexibility to either supplement the traditional Carrier Strike Group capability with that of an Expeditionary Strike Group, or even to combine an ESG alongside a CSG in order to mass combat capability into something like an expeditionary strike force. This provides the Navy-Marine Corps team with enhanced flexibility and lethality on the kill web chessboard."

The sixth takeaway is that MAWTS-1 overall and the F-35 part of MAWTS-1 are clearly focusing on the integrated distributed force and how the Marines can both leverage an overall joint and coalition force able to operate in such a manner as well as how the Marines can maximize their contribution to the integrated distributed force.

According to Major Hansell, the CO of MAWTS-1, Colonel Gillette has put a priority on how to integrate as best as we can with the Navy, as well as the joint force. "And for the F-35 period of instruction during all Weapons Schools, we focus a tremendous amount of effort on integrating with the joint force, more so than I ever did on a legacy platform. We really strive to make our graduates joint integrators, as well as naval integrators. And I give Colonel

Gillette all the credit in the world for moving us to that mindset and pushing us to learn how to operate in the evolving expeditionary environment."

Expeditionary Basing and C2

June 14, 2020

A key element of the challenge for successful mobile or expeditionary basing, which must be met is the command and control required to operate a distributed force which is integratable with the appropriate air-maritime force. This allows the expeditionary force both to make its maximal contribution to operations as well as to enhance its survivability.

Maj Tywan Turner Sr., TACC Division Head, Marine Aviation Weapons and Tactics Squadron 1 provided significant insights with regard to the C2 challenge. The Tactical Air Command Center, or TACC, provides oversight and direction of aerial battles and aircraft movement in an operational environment and at WTI plays a key role in integrating aviation assets from the West Coast, East Coast, and overseas.

The DI effort is a central piece of working C2 for mobile basing. The legacy approach has been to make C2 and ISR capabilities inherent to specific platforms, and then the task is to do after market integration and to work these disparate platforms together for operations. And during the land wars, the size of the C2 capabilities evolved over time, but the reduction in size of the servers is providing a significant opportunity to bring C2 to the tactical edge as well.

Moving forward, combing enhanced DI with much smaller footprint server capabilities to manage C2 data will provide a way ahead for working to deploy more efficacious expeditionary deployable C2.

The Aviation Command and Control System is referred to as "Common" because all MACCS agencies either have or are planning to adopt the software and equipment suite. But the baseline Common Aviation Command and Control System (CAC2S) during the land wars has operated from a Humvee frame, which obviously is not the best way to work the ship to shore concepts of operations which expeditionary C2 will require.

As Major Turner put it: "We need a smaller mousetrap to do C2 in the expeditionary basing environment." The Marines are working with a CAC2S smaller form factor to meet the evolving needs for force insertion. They are experimenting with decreasing the footprint of the server-software configuration to make it more deployable and overcome mobility and sustainment limitation (lift required, power requirements & fuel, cooling).

According to Major Turner: "CAC2S small-form factor SFF, has also shown early promise in being incorporated aboard naval vessels." It could provide enhanced DI between expeditionary bases and Naval strike groups as well. With regard to working the CAC2S deployable system, a correlated effort is working new ways to handle the wave forms which the ashore force would need in a variety of expeditionary environments.

And along with this effort, clearly signature management is a key consideration as well. A key part of the C2 effort is to enable the wave forms which need to be deployed with an expeditionary basing force, for those wave forms will determine with which force elements the Marines can integrate both to achieve their mission and to support the broader integrated distributable force. Clearly, a major challenge facing USMC-USN integrability revolves precisely around how best to ensure integratable C2.

Are the Marines decision makers operating from expeditionary bases or are they nodes in a fire control network? With the new computational technologies, which allow for the enablement of the internet of things at the tactical edge, the capability for the Marines to play the decision-making role with an extended kill web can be emphasized and enhanced going forward.

For the Marines to play a decision-making role from mobile basing, there is a key challenge as well associated with the evolution of the wave forms enabling deployed integrability. There needs to be management of the various wave forms to deliver what one might call a 360-degree waveform delivery system to the deployed Marines, to have both the SA as well as the decision space to support the proper scheme of maneuver from the mobile base.

By 360 degree, I am referring to an ability to manage wave forms which provide management of the ship to shore to airborne platform space to deliver the kill web effect. Such a 360-degree solution should also support all-domain access (specifically the space and cyberspace domains) to information that is normally held at the operational level. If the Marines are deploying strike teams to expeditionary basing, how best to ensure that they have the 360-degree waveform capability to achieve mission success?

The Evolving Amphibious Task Force

June 4, 2020

With the return to the sea on which the USMC has been working with the USN over the past few years, the role of "amphibiosity" has been in evolution as well. The Bold Alligator Exercises started in 2011 and re-focused on the importance of the return to the sea, *The Second Line of Defense* team attended Bold Alligator exercises and we have written several articles about those exercises. In effect, the evolution was crafted around the coming of the Osprey and under the influence of the coming of the F-35.

Put in blunt terms, it was about the Marines moving from a significant focus on the land wars to a "return to the sea." It is one in which the force would change from a primary role of providing a greyhound bus to insert force to an engagement force able to operate from the sea. It has involved shaping and understanding what an air-mobile force could do when able to operate at greater reach into littoral regions with a rapid insertion force. And one empowered by the Ospreys coupled with fifth-generation capability.

Under the twin influence of these two assets, the new LHA Class, the *USS America* ships, was introduced and with it, significantly different capabilities for the amphibious force itself. As the USN reworks how it is operating as a distributed maritime force, which is being reshaped around the capability to operate a kill web force, the question of how best to leverage and evolve the amphibious force is a key part of that transition itself. This is a work in progress, and one in which a determination of various paths to the future are in evolution, and will be subject to debate as well. Part of that evolution are changes in other elements of the amphibious task force which can over time play roles different from how various "legacy" platforms can be reworked to provide for new or expanded capabilities for the USN overall.

A case in point is how the Viper attack aircraft can evolve its roles AT SEA with the addition of key elements being generated by the DI effort, as well as adding a new weapons capability to the Viper, namely, the replacement for the Hellfire missile by the Joint Air-to-Ground Missile (JAGM) missile.

What this means is that the Viper can be a key part of the defense of the fleet while embarked on a variety of ships operating either independently, or as part of an amphibious task force. Because the Viper can land on and operate from of a wide range of ships, thus enabling operational and logistical flexibility, and with integration of Link 16 and full motion wave forms as part of DI improvements, the Viper can become a key member of the kill web force at sea.

In discussions in the Spring of 2020 with Major Thomas Duff and Mr. Michael Manifor, HQMC Aviation, APW-53, Attack and Utility Helicopter Coordinators, I learned of the evolving mission sets that Viper was capable of performing with the DI upgrades. "With the upgrades coming soon via the DI initiative, the Viper through its Link 16 upgrade along with its Full-Motion video access upgrade, can have access to a much wider SA capability which obviously enhances both its organic targeting capability and its ability to work with a larger swath of integrated combat space. This means that the Viper can broaden its ability to support other air platforms for an air-to-air mission set, or the ground combat commander, or in the maritime space… Because it is fully marinized, it can land and refuel with virtually any ship operating in the fleet, which means it can contribute to sea control, which in my view, is a mission which the amphibious task force will engage in with the expanded reach of adversarial navies."[19]

---

19   Robbin Laird, "Digital Interoperability and Kill Web Perspective for Platform Modernization: The Case of the Viper Attack Helicopter," *Second Line of Defense* (Jun 16, 2020).

Prior to my visit to MAWTS-1 in September 2020, I had a chance to discuss with Major "IKE" White the AH-1Z Division Head at MAWTS-1, the evolution of Viper enabled by upgrades for fleet operations as well as its well-established role in supporting the ground maneuver force. In that conversation, there were a number of takeaways which highlighted potential ways ahead.

The first takeaway is that the Marine Corps' utility and attack helicopters have been part of integrated operations and escort tasks throughout the land wars and can bring that experience to bear in the return to the sea. The Viper and the Venom have provided airborne escorts for numerous Amphibious Ready Groups over the past decade, partnering with destroyers, MH-60 Sierra and MH-60 Romeo to protect amphibious warships as they transited contested waterways.

The second takeaway is the coming of the JAGM, which will enable significant strike capability for the maritime force in providing for both sea control and sea denial. This missile provides increased lethality through a dedicated maritime mode, enhanced moving target capability, and selectable fusing; providing capability against both fast attack craft and small surface combatants. Millimeter wave (MMW) guidance increases survivability by providing a true fire-and-forget capability, removing the requirement for a terminal laser. Coupled with the AIM-9 sidewinder, the Viper will be able to engage most threats to naval vessels. The Viper's flexibility will provide even the most lightly defended vessels with a complete air and surface defense capability.

The third takeaway is that by working integration of the MH-60 Romeo helicopter with Viper, the fleet would gain a significant defense at sea capability. Integration of the two helicopters within the amphibious task force would allow them to provide an integrated capability to screen and defend the flanks of the afloat force. The MH-60 crews are optimized to integrate into the Navy's command and control architecture, and with onboard sensors can help detect potential targets and direct Vipers to engage threats. The integration of Link-16 will make this effort even more seamless.

Clearly, integrating Romeos which fly onboard the amphibious class ships with the Viper would provide a significant enhancement of the flank defense capabilities for the amphibious task force. Working a Romeo/Viper package would affect the evolution of the Romeos as well that would fly off of the L class ships as well. And all of this, frees up other surface elements to support other missions at sea, rather than having to focus on defending the amphibs as greyhound buses.

The fourth takeaway is that clearly this new role would have to be accepted and trained for, but the USN needs to rethink how amphibious ships can operate in sea control and sea denial functions in any case. The enhanced efforts at DI within the USMC aviation force needs to be accompanied by upgrades of the elements of the amphibious task force with regard to C2/ISR capabilities as well. We are seeing MISR or Maritime ISR officers placed within the Carrier Strike Groups, but they could be proliferated more broadly within the fleet.

In short, the evolution of the Viper with DI and with a new weapons package can clearly contribute to the evolution of the amphibious task force as it embraces sea control and sea denial missions and these missions will be crucial to supporting insertion forces moving to ashore expeditionary bases as well.

The Ground Combat Element in the Pacific Reset

September 24, 2020

As the USMC works its relationship with the USN, a core focus is upon how the Marine Corps can provide for enhanced sea control and sea denial. A means to this end is an ability to move combat pieces on the chessboard of the extended battlespace. But where does the ground combat element fight into this scheme for maneuver?

During my visit to MAWTS-1 in September 2020, I had a chance to discuss this with several USMC officers involved in the current Weapons and Tactics Instructor Course. And training in the context of transition is no picnic. The key is to ensure that the USMC is combat capable today as it transitions to a new GCE that is lighter and more capable of tapping not into the air-maritime joint force, above and beyond what USMC integration provides. As Col. Gillette, the CO of MAWTS-1 put it: "So long as I've been in the Marine Corps and the way that it still currently is today, marine aviation exists to support the ground combat. That's why we exist. The idea that we travel light and that the aviation element within the MAGTAF provides or helps to provide the ground combat element with a significant capability is our legacy. We are now taking that legacy and adapting it. We are taking the traditional combat engagement where you have battalions maneuvering and aviation supporting that ground element, and we are moving it toward Sea Control, and Sea Denial missions. We are reimagining the potential of what the infantry does.

"That doesn't mean that they do that exclusively because, although I think that our focus in the Marine Corps, as the Commandant said, is shifting toward the Pacific that doesn't relegate or negate the requirement to be ready to respond to all of the other things that the Marine Corps does. It might be less of a focus, but I don't think that that negates our requirement to deal with a variety of core missions.

"It's a question of working the balance in the training continuum. What does an infantry battalion train to? Do they train to a more traditional battalion in the attack or in the defense and then how do I use my aviation assets to support either one of those types of operations?" As opposed to, "I might have to take an island, a piece of territory that we're going to use a mobile base, secure it so that we can continue to push chess pieces forward in the Pacific, in the Sea Control, Sea Denial end-state."

"Those are two very different kind of skill sets. If there's one thing that the Marine Corps is very good at it's being very versatile and being able to switch from one to the other on relatively short order. But in order to do that, you have to have a very dedicated and well thought out training continuum so that people can do both well, because if you say that you can do it the expectation is that you can do it well."

Obviously, this is a major challenge and during my visit to MAWTS-1 in September 2020, I had a chance to talk with Major Fitzsimmons, the Ground Combat Department Head at MAWTS-1, who clearly is facing the challenges which his CO outlined. So what is the future of the Ground Combat Element in a distributed Marine Corps force operating both in the blue waters and the littorals?

This is clearly a challenge being worked, with the GCE facing the challenge of dealing with more traditional tasks as well as adapting to the evolving reconfiguration for the maritime fight. And it is a major shift facing the GCE for sure. The GCE is shifting from its most recent experiences of fighting in the land wars as a primary mission to providing support to, in Major Fitzsimmons words, "a more amphibious distributed force operation. And in my view, this is a very big shift."

Major Fitzsimmons provided a very helpful entry point into this discussion by recalling the earlier work which the Marines had done with the Company Landing Teams. As Major Fitzsimmons put it: "The Company Landing Team was an experiment at how do we lighten the footprint of the force while still giving them the capabilities of what we see in larger forces today. To do that, we would leverage DI, connectivity, and reach back to weapon systems, to information, to targeting, to any of those capabilities that you generally see at some of the higher echelons that were not organic to an infantry company at that time. The challenge then is to ensure that the infantry company has access to those types of capabilities and mature the force."

What Major Fitzsimmons meant by maturing the force was discussed later in the conversation. He highlighted the importance of having Marines earlier in their career able to work with various elements of the joint force, because they would need to leverage those capabilities as part of the more distributed GCE.

The Company Landing Team experiment also raised questions about equipment and personnel "How do we reinforce the CLT and how do we augment it with enablers? How do we augment it or enhance it with more proficient and more experienced fires personnel? How do we augment it with small UAS capabilities? How do we augment and enhance it with DI? How do they communicate with their organic radios across multiple waveforms? Who are they talking to? What is their left and right for decisions? Do they have fires approval? Would the company commander have fires approval, or would he have to do what we were having to do in Afghanistan and Iraq, where I've got to call my boss and then the boss's boss, in order to get fires employed?"

With the introduction of the new Marine Corps Littoral regiment, it is clear that these aspects of the CLT experiment are relevant to the way ahead. As Col. Gillette noted: "We are shaping a new Marine Littoral Regiment, MLR, but we're still in the nascent stages of defining what are the critical tasks that something like that needs to be able to do and then how you train to it. How do we create not only the definition of the skill sets that we need to train large formations to, but then what venues must we have to train?"

Major Fitzsimmons is an infantry officer with fires experience at the company and battalion level, and clearly is focused on the key aspect of how you enable smaller and less organically capable forces in the extended battlespace and ensure that they have adequate fires to execute their missions. And in dealing with peer competitors, clearly the ability to link the GCE with fires requires the right kinds of communication capabilities. As Major Fitzsimmons put it: "We are going to have to be significantly more distributed and quieter with respect to our emissions signatures than we have in the past."

A major challenge facing the GCE is the range of adaptability that they will have to be able to deliver and operate with in the future. As Col. Gillette noted earlier, the variety of skill sets required will be varied and tailorable. "How to train to best deliver such capability?" As Major Fitzsimmons put it: "I think the biggest shock to my community is going to be the level of adaptability that we're going to have to be able to achieve. We are going to have to train smaller forces to operate more autonomously and to possess the ability to achieve effects on the battlefield previously created at higher echelons."

He focused as well on the tailorable aspect envisaged as well. "We will need to be tactically tailored to achieve whatever effect we need. It should be akin to a menu; based on the mission and the effects needed to shape the environment toward mission accomplishment, we will need this capability or that capability that may require each element to be manned and equipped differently." Then there is the challenge of the sustainability of the tailored force. How to ensure the logistics support for the distributed maritime focused USMC GCE?

In short, fighting with the force you have while you transition to a new one is a major challenge facing the trainers for the USMC going forward.

Blue Water Expeditionary Operations

September 27, 2020

As the USMC focuses on how it can best help the USN in the maritime fight, two key questions can be posed: "How is the Marine Corps going to contribute most effectively to the Pacific mission in terms of Sea Control and Sea Denial? And how to best contribute to the defensive and offensive operations affecting the SLOCs?" The focus on sea control and sea denial can be seen in the Black Widow ASW exercise held in the Fall of 2020 where the USS Wasp participated. But skill sets associated with sea control, sea denial, SLOC offense, and defense do not translate easily from the Middle East land wars. How then to shape the new skill sets? And what is the underlying combat architecture which shapes the approach around which skill sets can be identified?

These are not easy questions to answer or even to frame properly. But if you are the center for excellence for Marine Corps air-enabled operations you clearly need to find some sound answers, and to shape an effective way ahead. Currently, this is what MAWTS-1 is doing.

As the discussions this year with officers at MAWTS-1 have highlighted, there is a major focus on how to do expeditionary and mobile basing in new ways to support the maritime fight. A key element for an evolving combat architecture clearly is an ability to shape rapidly insertable infrastructure to support Marine air as it provides cover and support to the Marine Corps ground combat element. This clearly can be seen in the reworking of the approach of the Aviation Ground Support element within MAWTS-1 to training for the execution of the Forward Air Refueling Point mission.

During my visit to MAWTS-1 in early September 2020, I had a chance to continue an earlier discussion with Maj Steve Bancroft, Aviation Ground Support (AGS) Department Head, MAWTS-1, MCAS Yuma. In this discussion, it was very clear that the rethinking of how to do FARPs was part of a much broader shift in in combat architecture designed to enable the USMC to contribute more effectively to blue water expeditionary operations. The focus is not only on establishing FARPs but only to do them more rapidly, and to move them around the chess board of a blue water expeditionary space more rapidly. FARPs become not simply mobile assets, but chess pieces on a dynamic air-sea-ground expeditionary battlespace in the maritime environment.

Given this shift, Major Bancroft made the case that the AGS capability should become the seventh key function of USMC Aviation. He argued that the Marine Corps capability to provide for expeditionary basing was a core competence which the Marines brought to the joint force and that its value was going up as the other services recognized the importance of basing flexibility.

But even though a key contribution, AGS was still too much of a pick-up effort. AGS consists of seventy-eight MOSs or military operational specialties which means that when these Marines come to MAWTS-1 for a WTI, that they come together to work how to deliver the FARP capability. As Major Bancroft highlighted: "The Marine Wing Support Squadron is the broadest unit in the Marine Corps. When the students come to WTI, they will know a portion of aviation ground support, so the vast majority are coming and learning brand new skill sets, which they did not know that the Marine Corps has. They come to learn new functions and new skill sets."

His point was rather clear: if the Marines are going to emphasize mobile and expeditionary basing, and to do so in new ways, it would be important to change this approach. "I think aviation ground support, specifically FARP-ing, is one of the most unique functions the Marine Corps can provide to the broader military."

He underscored how he thought this skill set was becoming more important as well. "With regard to expeditionary basing, we need to have speed, accuracy and professionalism to deliver the kind of basing in support for the Naval task force afloat or ashore."

With the USMC developing the combat architecture for expeditionary base operations, distributed maritime operations, littoral operations in a contested environment and distributed takeoff-vertical landing operations, reworking how to execute FARP operations is a key aspect to operate effectively an integrated distributed force.

FARPs in the evolving combat architecture need to be rapidly deployable and highly mobile, maintain a small footprint, and emit at a low signature. While being able to operate independently they need to be capable of responding to dynamic tasking within a naval campaign. This means that one is shaping a spectrum of FARP capability as well, ranging from light to medium to heavy in terms of capability to support and be supported. At the low end or light end of the scale one would create an air point, which is an expeditionary base expected to operate for up to seventy-two hours at that air point. If the decision is made to keep that FARP there longer, an augmentation force would be provided and that would then become an air site.

Underlying the entire capability to provide for a FARP clearly is airlift, which means that the Ospreys, the Venoms, the CH-53s, and the KC130Js provide a key thread through delivering FARPs to enable expeditionary basing. This is why the question of airlift becomes a key one for the new combat architecture as well. And as well, reimagining how to use the amphibious fleet as Lilly pads in blue water operations is a key part of this effort as well. In effect, an ability to project FARPs throughout the blue water and littoral combat space supporting the integrated distributed force is a key way ahead.

The F-35 and USMC-US Navy Integration

September 29, 2020

During my visit to MAWTS-1 and to NAWDC, one clear instrument of their enhanced integration in the contested battlespace was rather obvious: The F-35 and its evolution as a global enterprise. With the F-35 coming to the large deck carrier, the strike syllabus has changed. With the F-35 pioneered by the USMC, with its naval aviators leading the way, new capabilities have been brought to the force in terms of integratability, mobile basing, and combat power from the sea on a wider variety afloat asset than simply the large deck carrier.

With MAWTS-1 this year, I have discussed two sets of related questions: "What is the way ahead with regard to mobile and expeditionary basing? And how can the USMC provide greater support for the maritime battle?" Specifically, during my visit to MAWTS-1 in September 2020, we focused on two core questions: "How is the Marine Corps going to contribute most effectively to the Pacific mission in terms of Sea Control and Sea Denial? And how to best contribute to the defensive and offensive operations affecting the SLOCs?"

During the visit, I continued the discussion with the Col Gillette, CO of MAWTS-1, an experienced F-35 pilot, whom I first met at Eglin AFB who then returned to YUMA and transitioned in the first F-35 operational squadron deployed to Japan. My colleague Ed Timperlake once characterized the coming of the F-35 global enterprise, or the ability of a wide range of U.S. service and allied air forces to integrated together over the extended combat space as the twenty-first-century "big blue blanket."

The "big blue blanket" for the USN in World War II referred to the very large fleet deployed throughout the Pacific to deal with the tyranny of distance. Such a fleet does not exist today nor will it. Airpower is the key to shaping today's "big blue blanket," with the F-35 global enterprise as a key enabler. As Col. Gillette put it: "It is not only a question of interoperability among the F-35 fleet, it is the ability to have common logistical and support in the region with your allies, flying the same aircraft with the same parts. And the big opportunity comes with regard to the information point I made earlier. We are in the early stages of exploiting what the F-35 force can provide in terms of information dominance in the Pacific, but the foundation has been laid. And when we highlight the F-35 as the twenty-first-century version of what the World War II Navy called the big blue blanket with the redundancy and the amount of information that could be utilized, it's pretty astonishing if you think about it. The challenge is to work the best ways to sort through the information resident in the F-35 force and then how do you utilize it in an effective and efficient way for the joint force. But the foundation is clearly there."

During my visit, I met with Major Shockley, an F-35 instructor pilot at MAWTS-1, whose most recent F-35 experience has been in the Pacific with the squadron in Japan. He reinforced Col. Gillette's point in terms of the ability of USMC F-35s to work with allied, USAF and USN F-35s as well to shape a SA and strike force which expanded the reach of the joint or coalition force.

Indeed, Major Shockley highlighted the impact of F35-B thinking on base mobility. The F-35As and F-35Cs have some advantages in terms of fuel, and then range and loitering time with regard to the B, notably with regard to the C. Because the force is so inherently integratable, how best to work the chessboard of conflict with regard to where the various F-35 pieces move on the chessboard. From this standpoint, he argued for the importance of shaping a "rolodex of basing locations" where F-35s could land and operate in a crisis.

He had in mind, not only what the very basing flexible B could provide but thinking through deployment of "expeditionary landing gear" to allow the A's and C's to operate over a wider range of temporary air bases as well. Here, he was referring to preparing locations with the gear to enable landing on shorter run "airfields" as well as the kind of modifications the Norwegians have done with their F-35s enabling them to land in winter conditions in the High North as well.

With the F-35B as well, a much wider range of afloat assets are being used to enable the F-35 as a "flying combat system" to operate and enable ISR, C2, and strike capabilities for the joint and coalition force. This is being demonstrated throughout the amphibious fleet, a fleet which can be refocused on sea control and sea denial rather than simply transporting force to the littorals.

A key consideration when highlighting what the F-35 as a wolfpack can bring to the force is deploying in the force multiples that make sense for the force. This rests upon how the combat systems are configured on that force. In simple terms, the integrated CNI systems operate through a multiple layer security system, allowing a four ship F-35 force to operate as one.

With the Block IV software coming into the fleet, now an eight ship F-35 force can operate similarly. This allows for wolfpack operations and with the ability of the reach of the F-35 into other joint or coalition F-35 force packages the data flowing into the F-35 and the C2 going out has a very significant reach and combat impact.

This is not widely known or understood but provides a significant driver of change to being able to operate and prevail in denied combat environments. Leveraging this capability is critical for combat success for the U.S. and allied forces in the Pacific. And my visits to NAWDC and MAWTs-1 certainly underscore that these warfighters get that.

Unmanned Air Systems and the USMC

October 22, 2020

In 2018, I published a chapter on the USMC's recent experience with unmanned air systems in the book edited by John Jackson, entitled, *One Nation Under Drones*.[20] I focused on the substantial experience they have accumulated with Scan Eagle and then with the Blackjack system. The

---

20   John E. Jackson, editor, *One Nation Under Drones: Legality, Morality, and Utility of Unmanned Combat Systems*, (USNI Press, 2018.)

primary use has been in terms of ISR in the land wars, but with the return to the sea and now the focus on how the Marines can best help the USN in the maritime fight, the focus has shifted to how to best use UASs in the maritime domain.

With the recent decision to cancel its MUX ship-based UAS to pursue a family of systems, the focus will be upon both land-based and sea-based UASs but not to combine these capabilities into a single air vehicle. As the then Deputy Commandant of Aviation, Lt. General Rudder put it:

"In the next ten years, the quickest way—the commandant wants to go quick on this—this quickest way will be some sort of land-based high-endurance that can be based and still be able to provide the surface force, the amphibious force the capabilities that we would call "quarterback," or some sort of node that can provide twenty-four hours on station time, it will have all the networking and early warning and electronic warfare capabilities that they require for that type of thing."[21]

But the path to do this is not an easy one. And it is a path which is not just about the technology, but it is about having the skill sets to use whatever system is developed, the connectivity so that the combat effect can be connected to the maneuver force, and to have communication links which have low latency, notably in the maritime fight.

During my visit to MAWTS-1 in early September 2020, I had a chance to talk with Captain Dean, an experienced UAS officer who is a UAS instructor pilot at MAWTS-1. We discussed a wide range of issues with regard to UAS within the USMC, but one comment he made really gets at the heart of the transition challenge: "What capabilities do we need to continue to bring to the future fight that we currently bring to the fight?" What this question highlights it there is no combat pause for the Marines—they need to be successful in the current range of combat situations, and to re-shape those capabilities for the combat architecture redesign underway.

---

21   Megan Eckstein, "Marines Ditch MUX-Ship-Based Drone to Pursue Large Land-Based UAS, Smaller Shipboard Vehicle," *USNI News* (March 10, 2020).

But what if this is not as significant and overlapping as one might wish? This is notably true with regard to UAS systems. In general terms, the UAS systems which have been dominant in the Middle East land wars have required significant manning, lift capability to move them around in the battlespace and are not low-latency communications systems. Although referred to as unmanned, they certainly are not so in terms of support, movement of exploitation systems, or how that data gets exploited.

There clearly is a UAS potential for the blue water and littoral engagement force but crafting very low demand support assets, with low latency communications are not here as of yet. And in the current fights ashore, UASs, like Blackjack provide important ISR enablement to the Ground Combat Element. And as the Marines have done so, they have gained very useful combat experience and shaping of relevant skill sets to the way ahead for the UAS within the future force.

The goal is to have more flexible payloads for the UAS force going forward, but that means bringing into the UAS world, experienced operators in fields broader than ISR, such as electronic warfare. But there is clearly a tension between funding and fielding of larger UAS's for the amphibious task force, and shaping new systems useable by combat teams. And the phrase about distributing information at the right time and at the right place sounds good, this is very difficult to do, given the need to ensure that the data links do not dangerously expose the combat force to adversary target identification.

This is yet another key area where contested combat space has not much to do with what one can do with UASs in uncontested air space. Captain Dean underscored that since 2015, "we have been able to normalize unmanned aviation with the USMC. We have been able to bring in a lot of experience into the VMUs (Unmanned Aerial Vehicle Squadrons) and with the sundowning of the Prowlers, have brought in Marines experienced with electronic warfare as well. We continue to prioritize our training on the Blackjacks going to the MEUs."

He highlighted that this posed a challenge for transition. For the Blackjacks operating off the amphibious force, changes need to be made on those ships to get full value from operating these UASs. But if the Blackjack is a short-term or mid-term solution, the kind of investment which needs to be made is not likely to happen. What he highlighted was the crucial importance of the infrastructure afloat to make best use of the UASs which the USMC and USN will operate. And given the challenge of managing space onboard the ship, sorting out the nature of the infrastructure and how to manage it is a key aspect of the way ahead for UASs.

Another challenge is who wants what within the combat force. If we are looking at the fleet as a whole, the desire is to have fleet wide ISR, or capabilities to deliver combat effect. If one is focused on the battalion, they are focused on having capabilities organic to the battalion itself.

Again, this is a development and investment challenge which as well raises questions of what kind of infrastructure can be developed to deal with each of these different operational level requirements. "What does the MAGTF want? What does the battalion want? These are not the same things."

In short, a key question facing the Marines with regard to UASs: "What capabilities do we need to continue to bring to the future fight that we currently bring to the fight?"

CHAPTER FIVE

THE PERSPECTIVE OF THE U.S. NAVY'S AIR BOSS

"Training, Training, Training"

October 12, 2019

As Admiral Nimitz confronted the last century's challenges in the Pacific, he concluded a core lesson for this century's Pacific warriors: "Having confronted the Imperial Japanese Navy's skill, energy, persistence, and courage, Nimitz identified the key to victory: 'training, TRAINING and M-O-R-E T-R-A-I-N-I-N-G.'"[22]

The United States and its core allies are shaping new capabilities to deal with the various threats and challenges in the Pacific in the time of the Asian century. Flexibility in operations and agility in inserting force with a proper calibration of effect will be enhanced as new systems come on line in the years ahead. But these systems will have the proper effect only in the hands of skilled warriors.

In a visit in the Fall of 2019 to Naval Air Station, North Island, in San Diego, to meet with VADM Miller, Commander Naval Air Forces, or the "Air Boss" of the USN, we focused on the training challenge. Joining the discussion was the F-35 U.S. Navy Wing Commander, Captain Max McCoy. We discussed the evolution of the Naval Air Wings in the context of the Navy working its way forward toward a kill web enabled force.

---

22   James D. Hornfischer, *Neptune's Inferno: The U.S, Navy at Guadalcanal* (Bantam, 2012), chapter 44.

VADM Miller started by underscoring that significant change is underway for the carrier air wing or CAG. The F-35 is providing a forcing function of change. According to VADM Miller: "fifth-generation capability is a catalyst for change: how we fight, how we train, how we maintain and sustain aircraft, how we flight test, and how man our squadrons (pilots and maintenance personnel). The emphasis is interoperability, networking, distributed forces, and integration."

But several new capabilities are being introduced into the operational force, such as the Triton, P-8s, modernized Super Hornets, the new Hawkeye, and the MQ-25 unmanned tanker. These new capabilities are being worked into an evolving Naval strike force to shape new capabilities for the carrier and for the distributed force.

Captain Max McCoy highlighted what one might call the forcing function of the F-35 and of the F-35 aviators upon the training dynamic. "We are teaching F-35C pilots to be wingmen but training them to think like mission commanders. F-35C provides more SA than ever before and pilots must be able to influence the battlespace both kinetically and non-kinetically. The pilot must interpret cockpit information and determine the best means to ensure mission success either through his own actions or by networking to a distributed force."

The F-35 pilots need to think like mission commanders, in which they are operating in terms of both leveraging and contributing to the networked force. This means that the skill sets being learned are not the classic TTPs for a combat pilot but are focused on learning how to empower and leverage an integrated force. "Training can no longer focus solely on T/M/S capabilities. Training has to develop young aviators who appreciate their role within a larger maneuver/combat element. Specifically, how does F-35C complement fourth-generation capabilities within the Carrier Air Wing and surface combatants distributed within the Carrier Strike Group?"

Captain McCoy continued: "It is no longer about fighting as a section or division of fighter aircraft. We only win if we fight as an interoperable, networked, and distributed force. We are still learning and incorporating fifth-generation capability into the Navy. Our efforts must be calculated and measured but push beyond historical comfort zones. We must embrace what is new and redefine what is basic warfighting capability. This starts with the Fleet Replacement Squadron (FRS) and Air Combat Training Continuum (ACTC) syllabi. We must make integrated training a key component of a pilot's progression from FRS graduate to mission commander. F-35C is an enabler, if and only if, we train our pilots to think well beyond the limits of their cockpit and reach of an individual aircraft's weapons system".

They are learning how to operate as distributed force packages. This is leading to radical disjuncture from traditional training approaches and thinking. How do you best train your aviators to tap into networks and provide for distributed strike? In shifting from a training focus on traditional TTPs, how do Naval aviator's problem solve differently? How to reshape effectively the infrastructure to support new training approaches? How do Naval aviators integrate with and maximize their impact for and on the combat force?

Live Virtual Constructive Training provides a technological path but is a necessary but not sufficient tool set for the Navy to get where they need to go. Training is now about shaping domain knowledge for the operational force to ensure that "we can be as good as we can be all of the time."

According to Vice Admiral Miller: "The ability to reshape training and change culture requires a warfighting community to break from traditional training methods either on the range, at sea and in the simulated environment. There are numerous reasons why we must find a new balance among live, virtual and constructive (LVC) training in a distributed mission training (DMT) construct. Range infrastructure, threat simulation, cost to operate, and security are driving us to search for new training opportunities.

"However, the most important reason is operational readiness—warfighting first. We must be ready and prepared to fight at all times…. We need to be focused on force integration among fourth- and fifth-generation aircraft while also providing the medium to integrate with surface combatants."

Captain McCoy added: "Again, in the future, we are all wingmen in the battlespace who must think well beyond the cockpit or bridge of our platforms. LVC/DMT will be the proving ground that unlocks how we think and encourages TTP development that would otherwise be hindered by fiscal constraints and under-resourced or inadequate ranges. It is the bridge that builds cooperation and cohesiveness among communities. LVC/DMT is the common ground that teaches our amazing tacticians how to appreciate a wide range of capabilities that are far more effective in the collective."

If Admiral Nimitz would visit Naval Air Station, North Island, today, he would be amazed and pleased to see the technology in the hands and coming into the hands of the Naval aviation community. But he certainly would wish to see the twenty-first-century re-set of training underway to be fully supported and funded.

The Integratable Air Wing

March 13, 2020

The USN over the next decade will reshape its CVW with the introduction of a number of new platforms. If one simply lists the initial operating capabilities of each of these new platforms, and looked at their introduction sequentially, the "air wing of the future" would be viewed in additive terms— what has been added and what has been subtracted and the sum of these activities would be the carrier air wing of the future.

But such a graphic and such an optic would miss the underlying transformation under way, one which is highly interactive with the USMC and the USAF. One clearly needs a different optic or perspective than simply taking an additive approach. What is underway is a shift from integrating the air wing around relatively modest and sequential modernization efforts for the core platforms to a robust transformation process in which new assets enter the force and create a swirl of transformation opportunities, challenges, and pressures. How might we take this new asset and expand the reach and effectiveness of the carrier strike group? How might it empower maritime, air, and ground forces as we shape a more effective (i.e. a more integratable) force?

During a visit to San Diego in February 2020, I had a chance to discuss such an evolving perspective with the Navy's Air Boss, Vice Admiral "Bullet" Miller. We started by discussing the F-35 which for him is a major forcing function change in the CVW. But his focus is clearly upon not simply introducing the aircraft into the force but ensuring that it is part of the launch of a transformative process for shaping the evolving air wing or what I call F-35 2.0. The F-35 is coming to the force after a significant investment and work by the USN to rebuild its operational capabilities after several years of significant sustainment challenges. But now the Air Boss is looking to focus his attention on enhanced combat lethality which the fleet can deliver to the maritime services and the joint force.

What is being set in motion is a new approach where each new platform which comes into the force might be considered at the center of a cluster of changes. The change is not just about integrating a new platform in the flight ops of the carrier. The change is also about how the new platform affects what one can do with adjacent assets in the CSG or how to integrate with adjacent United States or allied combat platforms, forces, and capabilities.

Vice Admiral Miller provided several examples of how this shift affects the thinking about new platforms coming onboard the carrier deck. One such example is the new unmanned tanker, the MQ-25. The introduction of this new air asset will have an immediate effect in freeing up fourth-generation fighters, currently being used for tanking, to return to their strike role. Even more importantly from a transformation perspective, the MQ-25 will have operational effects as a platform which will extend the reach and range of the CVW.

But MQ-25 will be a stakeholder in the evolving C2/ISR capabilities empowering the entire combat force, part of what, in my view, is really sixth-generation capabilities, namely, enhancing the power to distribute and integrate a force as well as to operate more effectively at the tactical edge. The MQ-25 will entail changes to the legacy air fleet, changes in the con-ops of the entire CVW and trigger further changes with regard to how the C2/ISR dynamic shapes the evolution of the CVW and the joint force.

The systems to be put onto the MQ-25 will be driven by overall changes in the C2/ISR force. These changes are driving significant improvements in size, capability, and integration, so much so that it is the nascent sixth gen. This means that the USN can buy into "6th gen" by making sure that the MQ-25 can leverage the sensor fusion and the integrated CNI systems on the F-35 operating as an integrated force with significant outreach. It is important to realize that a four-ship formation of an F-35 operating as an integrated man–machine-based sensor fusion aircraft operates together as a four-ship pack fully integrated through the CNI system, and as such can provide a significant driver of change to the overall combat force.

Not only does this affect the future of training but also how operations, training, and development affect individual platforms once integrated into the CVW and larger joint force.

A key piece in shaping the integratable air wing is building out a new training capability at Fallon and a new set of working relationships with other United States and allied training centers. The head of Fallon, Rear Admiral Richard Brophy, joined the conversation with the Air Boss, and clearly underscored the challenge: "How do we best train the most lethal integrated air wing preparing to deploy, but at same time, prepare for the significant changes which introducing new platforms and concepts of operations can bring to the force?"

As the Air Boss put it: "We need properly to train the integratable airwing and we are investing in expanded ranges and new approaches such as Live Virtual Constructive training. I often use the quote that 'your performance in combat never raises to the level of your expectations but rather it falls to the level of your training.' This is why the training piece is so central to the development for the way ahead for the integrable training. It is not just about learning what we have done; but it is working the path to what we can do."

Consider the template of training for CVW integration. On the one hand, the CVW trained at Fallon needs to prepare to go out into the fleet and deliver the capabilities that are available for today's fight. On the other hand, as this template is executed, it is important to shape an evolving vision on how to operate platforms coming to the fleet or how those assets have already been modified by software upgrades.

A software upgradeable fleet, which is at the heart of the fifth-gen transition and which lays down the foundation for sixth-generation C2/ISR, provides a key challenge. The F-35 which operated from the last carrier cycle, or flew with the P-8 or Triton, all of these assets might well have new capabilities delivered by the software development cycle. How to make certain that not just the air wing, but the commanders at sea fully understand what has changed. The challenge is to shape the template for training today's fleet; and to ensure that the template being shaped has an open aperture to handle the evolution of the CVW into the evolving integrated and distributed force.

A measure of and symbol of change is the new Maritime ISR or MISR patch. MISR officers are trained as ISR subject matter experts to operate at the fleet or CSG level and to work the sensor fusion for the integratable CVW. According to the Air Boss: "I think of MISR as additive, not lessening of TOPGUN, but instead akin to a new phase which builds upon our historical experience in the development of TOPGUN in the first place." In effect, these are "sixth-generation officers" in the sense of working the C2/ISR capabilities which enable an integrated and distributed fleet to have its maximum combat impact.

In short, the fleet is in the throes of significant transition and with it the role, scope and focus of the training effort and mission.

An Update on the Integratable Air Wing
July 23, 2020

During a visit to North Island in July 2020, I had a chance to continue the discussion with the Air Boss about shaping a way ahead for training and fleet innovation. At the meeting with the Air Boss, either in person or in the teleconference, was my host for the NAWDC visit and the CO of NAWDC, Rear Admiral Rich Brophy; the Chief of Staff for the Air Boss, Captain Max McCoy, most recently, head of the Navy's operational F-35C force; and the head of the N98 requirements division as well as the N98 officer involved with the MQ-25-program.

What was clear from visiting NAWDC, and from my prior discussions with the heads of the weapons training departments at NAWDC, is that the training center is focused on the integratable air wing, and the role of carrier aviation working more broadly with the fleet and the joint force. Two new warfighting departments have been put in place which represent the shift— namely, the MISR Weapons School and the information warfare department, which is focused on the challenge of dynamic targeting.

At NAWDC, there is a significant shift from a primary focus on TTPs for platforms and their integration on the carrier to a focus on TTPs for broader functional areas wherein TTPs need to be shaped fleet wide, such as for joint maritime strike. With regard to MISR WTIs, their core task is to work integrability between organic carrier ISR assets with non-organic ISR assets and sensors to assist in the process of CSG decision-making, and in the case of assignment to the fleet level, to do so for the fleet decision makers.

This obviously is a fundamental shift and a work in progress. The impact of the F-35 is part of the process of change. Currently at NAWDC, an F-35C squadron is working closely with the Hawkeye community to shape the kind of integrability which could flow nicely into the expanded reach of the fleet to deliver the combat effects necessary for either the high-end fight or full spectrum crisis management.

But more generally with regard to MISR contributions, clearly the focus has been, as Vice Admiral Miller put it: "Build the capability and they will come" with regard to the recognition of the growing contributions of the sensor network and evolving C2 to fleet innovation.

Another case in point has been the coming of the Triton to Pacific operations. The Triton brings a whole new layer of SA and targeting capabilities to the fleet, and with the growing awareness of the priority on integration of the USAF with Navy fleet operations, the Triton can provide a contribution to the integrability of the two services as well. Indeed, the USAF and the USN are engaging in a clear effort to better integrate across the board, notably with regard to bombers and the fleet. The USN is hosting an exercise called RESOLUTE HUNTER which is working ways to better integrate ISR, C2, and Battle Management across the forces, with the next iteration to be held this November.

Looking Back

September 9, 2020

In my discussion with Vice Admiral Miller in February, 2020, we discussed the way ahead for the carrier air wing. In that conversation, we highlighted the way ahead for the carrier wing in terms of a shift from the integrated to the integratable air wing. The shift is a significant one in which the carrier air wing is reaching out beyond what is on the carrier organically to what it can tap into in the broader joint and coalition force kill web capabilities. It is about how the carrier wing can both be supported and support an integrated distributed force.

And my recent visit to the Naval Air Warfare Development Center, focused on a significant development which highlighted the new way ahead. At Fallon Naval Air Station, the NAWDC team is working fleet wide and expanding working relationships with the USAF and USMC to shape TTPs for the fleet in the high-end fight. For example, NAWDC chaired a working group earlier this year on how the fleet can work together to shape integrated maritime strike operations.

During his almost three-year tenure as Air Boss, Vice Admiral Miller worked with his team to set in motion a solid foundation for this transition. In an interview on September 3, 2020 in his office at North Island Naval Air Station, San Diego, we had a chance to discuss the challenges which he and his team has faced during his tenure.

Question: What are the biggest challenges you faced when you became the Air Boss?

Vice Admiral Miller: "There were three main things when I came in, and most of them were near term focused. Readiness was unacceptable. For example, 50% of our FA-18s weren't flyable. Readiness was clearly the first and the highest priority. The second one was to shift our training from counter-terrorism to what we need to fight and win a great power competition. The third involved manning challenges. We had gotten ourselves to where we had no bench. We were putting our combat teams together right at the end game and sending them out the door on deployment, and we really weren't cultivating the expertise we need for the high-end fight. We knew that meeting these challenges was not an overnight challenge but required a sustained effort…."

Question: I have seen the training changes, which are significant at Jax Navy, Mayport and at NAWDC. How would describe the training reset and refocus?

Vice Admiral Miller: "The key focus has been upon a complete reworking at Fallon. We have totally revamped the strike syllabus, for example. We have migrated the new approach into all of our workups, unit level workups, our advanced readiness programs…

"New training and new assets mean new training to work integration for the fleet. We will continue to evolve as our weapons systems evolve, to include MQ-25 and what it's going to bring to the Carrier Strike Group in the middle of the decade. We're already starting to think about how we need to train as the carrier air wing evolves. We're also making great strides as far as live virtual constructive and how we connect everything from our simulation capability to what we're able to do out on the ranges.

"The one area that's going to be a big issue for us this year, especially in Congress, is going to be the Fallon range expansion. With the changing nature of warfare, we need to change not just our training approach but the ranges on which we prepare for combat…"

Question: Another challenge clearly is when you add new platforms, how do you get the operators to think past their legacy platform to what they are now flying. How significant has been that problem?

Vice Admiral Miller: "This is a challenge, getting P-3 operators not to operate in the "alone and unafraid" mentality of their legacy aircraft, to what the P-8, Triton, Romeo synergy delivers to the fleet. This is a major training opportunity and challenge. We need to take advantage of the leaps in technology that we had as we modernize."

CONCLUSION

During my visit to NAWDC in July 2020, I was able to talk with Rear Admiral Brophy and his senior officers throughout the week of my visit, to get an update with regard to how the USN aviation community is addressing the training environment for the high-end fight. And given that NAWDC is hosting a number of working groups Navy-wide and joint force wide to rethink, reimagine and rework the role of the fleet, it is an epicenter for driving change.

As Rear Admiral Brophy put it: "Admiral Miller gave me the following charge when I took command: 'Snap', when you go there get us in a great power competition mindset. From a wholly integrated perspective, look at what we need to do at NAWDC in order to win the next fight." And to do this he emphasized that my job was to pursue holistic training with the Navy and to work with other US warfighting centers and key allies."

To be blunt: this is not easy, and entails opening the aperture on what Naval Aviation is training to do, and how it will work more effectively with not just USN "owned" assets but those most relevant to operations against adversary forces operating in a contested battlespace. What this means in blunt terms is that the USN is moving from its support to the land forces engaged in conflict in the Middle East as a key mission set, to returning to priority focus on blue water operations, and naval warfare, but in a twenty-first-century focus.

It is far easier to write these words, than to understand actually what they mean. And if one goes to MAWTS-1 which is not that far to fly to when operating as a Naval operator, which both the Marine and Naval aviators are, one sees how significant the shift to operating in the maritime domain against a high-end competitor is from both the operating and training perspective.

What is clearly crucial to understand is that training and its impacts are changing fundamentally under the impact of twenty-first-century technologies. Having discussed the shift with both Marine Corps and Naval officers this year and having visited both premier training centers, I would draw a number of conclusions.

First, the Navy and Marine Corps are focusing on how significantly to reset the capabilities of the current force, or the force they have today. It is not about force design in 2030, 2040, or the world in 2050.

Second, both are looking to shape new skill sets to use that force much more effectively.

Third, both are preparing to use new platforms which will come into the force to enhance the kinds of capabilities needed for the contested battlespace. Put a different way, they are reshaping their skill sets with the force they have and are doing so with full anticipation of new platforms and capabilities coming into the force.

Fourth, both warfighting training centers are in the process of reshaping their training tools and approaches to forge their ways ahead in the joint fight.

Fifth, officers of both warfighting centers are acutely aware of shortfalls in current force capabilities and are working ways to inform force development efforts to close gaps, which they deem crucial rather than just buy new things. This is especially true with regards to weapons acquisition and development. By addressing the maritime engagement, it is clear that the stockpiles are too low and the inventory is too focused on high end strike assets.

It is clear that there needs to a significant shift towards building out a strike force which is empowered by a wide range of tools for lethality, both non-kinetic and kinetic. For example, the threat of swarming drones is clearly on the horizon. But how well do swarming drones do when confronted with relatively lower end munitions such as delivered by Viper attack helicopter, namely, its guns and its laser guided munitions?

Sixth, new methods of training are clearly required to guide ways ahead to reshape the force for the high-end fight, and this is not well captured by phrases bandied about by the training community such as live virtual constructive training. There is no single technology for training, synthetic or not that can fill the training gaps being opened up by the high-end training community.

Seventh, a key advantage of the U.S. warfighter is initiative of the deployed warfighter, rather than the top-down commander dominating the actions to be taken in the battlespace. And a clear challenge will be to find ways to empower the distributed force able to operate in a flexible integrated manner to deliver decisive effect.

In short, significant change is underway but such change is not easily captured by the cubical commandos. But this is a work in progress, and this work will succeed only if the repairs of the readiness shortfalls only recently put in place are maintained.

To train for and execute the capabilities of the high-end fight requires that training and exercises be well funded, and the innovation being generated by the warfighting centers drive force structure development. The force that is evolving is a very capable one, but the reset in its combat approaches and combat architecture are crucial to enhancing its capabilities to provide for the kinds of escalation management and skills need for the world we are now in.

ABOUT THE AUTHOR

A long-time analyst of global defense issues, Dr. Robbin F. Laird has worked in the U.S. Government and several think tanks, including the Center for Naval Analysis and the Institute for Defense Analysis. He is a Columbia University alumnus, where he taught and worked for several years at the Research Institute of International Change, a think tank founded by Dr. Brzezinski. He is a frequent op-ed contributor to the defense press, and he has written several books on international security issues.

Dr. Laird has taught at Columbia University, Queens College, and Johns Hopkins University. He has received various academic research grants from various foundations, including the Fritz Thyssen Foundation, the United States Institute for Peace, etc.

He is the editor of two websites, *Second Line of Defense* and *Defense. info*. He is a member of the Board of Contributors of *Breaking Defense* and publishes there on a regular basis. He is a regular contributor to *FrontLine Defence* as well.

He is a frequent visitor to Australia where he is a Research Fellow with The Williams Foundation in supporting their seminars on the transformation of the Australian Defence Force. Recently, he has become a Research Fellow with The Institute for Integrated Economic Research-Australia. The Institute is focused on a number of key macro social/defense issues that revolve around establishing trusted supply chains and resiliency in dealing with the challenges posed by the twenty-first-century authoritarian powers. The work has been captured in his recent book *Joint by Design: The Evolution of Australian Defence Strategy*.

He also is based in Paris, France from where he has frequently visited military and foreign policy officials as well as military bases within Europe as a whole and has recently co-authored a book with Murielle Delaporte titled *The Return of Direct Defense in Europe: Meeting the 21st Century Authoritarian Challenge.*

RECENT SECOND LINE OF DEFENSE BOOKS

The Return of Direct Defense in Europe: Meeting the 21st Century Authoritarian Challenge

Published in e-book in October, 2020, and the paperback in December, 2020, the co-authors, Robbin F. Laird and Murielle Delaporte, focus on how the liberal democracies are addressing the challenges of the 21st century authoritarian powers, in terms of their evolving approaches and capabilities to deal with their direct defense.

As General (Rtd.) Jean-Paul Paloméros, former NATO Commander and head of the Allied Transformation Command put it with regard to the book: "One of the many great values of *The Return of Direct Defense in Europe* is that (it addresses directly the need) to meet the challenge of XXIst century authoritarian powers. Because the great risks that lie in front of our democracies deserve to be named: national selfishness, divergence of strategic and economic interests, trampling on fundamental and commonly agreed values.

"*The Return of Direct Defense in Europe* is both a moving testimony to those who have built and defended our democracies for seven decades but as well a vibrant appeal to resurrect the spirit and the will of the democratic Alliance's founding fathers.

"It's true that the future is unpredictable, but nevertheless, it's our permanent duty to prepare for it and to learn from our history: as the Spanish-born U.S. philosopher George Santayana (1863-1952) put it: "those who cannot remember the past are condemned to repeat it."

"In writing this outstanding tribute to democracies and the crucial need to keep on fighting for their values, Robbin Laird and Murielle Delaporte do not only draw a very well informed and instructive historic perspective on the defense of Europe since the Second World War.

"They enlighten as well with regard to the crucial challenges of the present and even more of the future, with regard to the key choices that leaders of our democracies must make, and with regard to the key question that lies in front of new generations: How best to defend together democracy as a unique heritage built upon the sacrifices of their fathers?"

Professor Kenneth Maxwell underscored: "This is a fascinating and very timely account of the major shifts and challenges which have transformed post–Cold War Europe and outlines in troubling detail the formidable challenges which lie ahead in the post-COVID-19 pandemic world. It is essential reading for all those who forget that history must inform the present.

"It illustrates the need for a hard-headed evaluation of the continuities as well as the ruptures of the recent past which has transformed both the scope of North Atlantic Treaty Organization (NATO) and the European Community, and which has also created opportunities for enemies of democratic government to thrive in a resurgent Russia under the leadership of Vladimir Putin. These challenges will not go away any time soon."

Joint by Design: The Evolution of Australian Defence Strategy

In the midst of the COVID-19 crisis, the prime minister of Australia, Scott Morrison, launched a new defense and security strategy for Australia. This strategy reset puts Australia on the path of enhanced defense capabilities. The change represents a serious shift in its policies towards China, and in reworking alliance relationships going forward. *Joint by Design* is focused on Australian policy, but it is about preparing liberal democracies around the world for the challenges of the future.

The strategic shift from land wars to full spectrum crisis management requires liberal democracies to have forces lethal enough, survivable enough, and agile enough to support full spectrum crisis management. The book provides an overview of the evolution of Australian defence modernization over the past seven years, and the strategic shift underway to do precisely that.

Published in e-book at the end of 2020, with a hardback and paperback to be released in the first quarter of 2021, *Joint By Design* provides a unique perspective on how senior Australian defence officials have reworked with their political leadership the transformation of their forces and are rethinking the focus of their strategy.

2020: A Pivotal Year?
Navigating Strategic Change at a Time of COVID-19 Disruption

This book focuses on the impact of COVID-19 and strategic change evidenced in 2020. The book incorporates a number of essays and articles from our two major websites, *Second Line of Defense* and *Defense Information*.

2020 was a unique year. We have brought together our essays and articles which highlights that uniqueness as well as focusing on a number of the strategic dynamics of 2020. In effect, the book is a reader which provides an overview on the challenge of navigating strategic change at a time of COVID-19 disruption.

The book is divided into six parts.

- The first part highlights our assessments of COVID-19 and its impact on defense and shaping a way ahead.

- The second part highlights a number of broader global dynamics of change, which include a variety of assessments of Brazil, the Pacific, and the Middle East.

- The third part highlights developments Europe-wide, and upon the Macron and Merkel leadership responses, traces a number of French policy developments and the challenges of dealing with the 21st century authoritarian democracies.

- The fourth part focuses on Australian developments, with the launching of a new defense strategy and a shift in Australian-Chinese relations.

- The fifth part highlights historical perspectives which provide some insights with regard to the way ahead as well.

- The sixth part provides a look ahead into 2021.

The book will be published in e-book in the first quarter of 2021 with a paperback to be released shortly thereafter.